A

GERMAN

LIFE

BY BERND WOLLSCHLAEGER, MD

EMOR PUBLISHING, LLC

A German Life

Against All Odds – Change Is Possible

Please visit our web site at www.agermanlife.com

Printed in the United States of America
Contributing Editors – Alan Adelson, Alan Anderson & Frank Blackwell

Cover design by Sierra Productions
1582 Deere Avenue, Irvine, CA 92606-4811
www.sierraproductions.com
Library of Congress Cataloging-in- Publication Data is available on request

ISBN-13: 978-0-9791831-0-2
ISB-10: 0-9791831-0-3

For information about special discounts for bulk purchases please contact
Emor Publishing
P.O. Box 6
Hollywood,FL 33022

FOR CHRISTA

I WANT TO THANK MY WIFE ROSE
AND MY CHILDREN TAL, JADE AND NATALIA
FOR THEIR ENCOURAGEMENT
AND UNCONDITIONAL LOVE
IN MY STRUGGLE FINDING INNER PEACE
AND SERENITY.

CONTENTS

A
GERMAN
LIFE

5/7/09

To Claire

yours

CHAPTER 1

IN THE BEGINNING

GERMANY, DECEMBER 24ᵀᴴ, 2004

ALTHOUGH IT HAD BEEN almost forty years, I remembered the way to the cemetery in Bamberg as though I had been there the day before. On my last visit, my mother had taken me to my grandparent's grave, and I remembered watching her as she stood silently in prayer, but I have no memory of my grandparents as people. My grandmother died when I was three, outliving my grandfather by several years. I remembered my mother's wishes to be buried next to her parents and therefore I knew that I would find her grave next to theirs and I assumed that my father would be buried there too. Now, on this visit to my parent's grave, I had no clue about what was expected of me, or what I expected of myself.

I parked the car at the entrance to the cemetery and sat silent for a moment.

"You want us to go with you?" my wife asked. I looked at her and glanced briefly at my five-year-old daughter in the back seat.

"I'll be okay. I think I have to do this alone. Thank you, though."

She nodded and smiled at me. I admit that I was afraid, but until that moment I had not allowed myself to reflect deeply enough on the death of my parents. It seemed extraordinary that I had successfully avoided confronting my feelings about them for all these years.

My father died a little less than six months after I left Germany, and my mother passed away a few years later. For many years I preferred to think they each died of a physical ailment, because that thought was somehow less painful for me to accept. More recently I had come to believe they each died of a broken heart. Whatever the cause, we never had time to say goodbye, and I sorely missed the closure of speaking with them at the end. Nor had I fully honored their memories, letting my anger and resentment block the way. Now I tried to face the reality that they were gone for good. I kept thinking of new questions I wanted to ask, of times when I should have tried harder to generate conversations with them, however awkward.

But they were gone now, my life had changed, and I was left with those questions forever, the answers to which I had to find for myself.

"I won't be long," I said as I left the car.

"Take your time," my wife said as I closed the door.

It was cold outside, and the sky was gray, quite typical for a German winter season.

A few snowflakes tumbling around in a slight, cold breeze.

I was barely aware of them as they settled on my face, leaving a streak of cold melted water that blended with the tears that were running down my face.

I walked through the gate and glanced at old and new gravestones carved with expressions of love and sorrow. Not consciously knowing where I was going, I followed my instincts, turning left and then right and then left again. I remembered that my grandparents' grave was close to a wall whose purpose was to separate the Christian graves from the Jewish cemetery.

Recognizing the wall, I scanned the gravestones for their names and suddenly found myself standing in front of them.

A simple gray marble stone with four names etched in dark color on the gray headstone.

I had never visited their grave since leaving Germany for Israel almost twenty years earlier.

At times I angrily rejected the notion of visiting their grave to pay respect to their memory, and I guess that I was not ready to do so. But so much had changed since then.

I was a father now, and loved my children, and they deserved answers about their family history, my life, and that of my parents and grandparents.

I finally disclosed my past to my son and he was so taken by my story that he decided to write an essay about it. That prompted his teacher to call me, inquiring about this fantastic story, and I decided to confide in the teacher. I was invited to speak to my son's class, and then his entire school. The act of revealing the truth had the effect of connecting me again to my parents and convinced me to return home after more than twenty years for this visit.

Standing in front of their grave I did not know how to respond to the powerful feelings surging through me, and I just stood there frozen in time.

On the headstone, my father's full name was followed by the symbol of the Knight's cross, indicating that a highly-decorated soldier was buried there. My mother's name was beneath his, and I spoke to both of them.

"Here I am," I mumbled into my frozen beard.

Choking on the only words I could manage to whisper, I closed my eyes to visualize their faces. I remembered the last time we were together, when I hugged my mother.

She was holding me tightly, probably knowing that we would never see each other again.

I thought it would be difficult to remember my father after so many years, but his stern gaze and dark eyes flashed into my memory with unmistakable power.

My mind was flooded with flashbacks of our times together: fishing and hunting trips in beautiful forests, along the blue rivers and lakes in Bavaria; long walks together on Sunday mornings; the lively debates about life and politics. The memories came rushing back so vividly that I could almost hear our voices. I could even remember the smell of my mother's perfume, my father's violent eruptions of anger and aggression, his dependence on alcohol and his failing attempts to control his drinking.

I remember, most of all, my conflicting feelings toward his military career and his long service in the German Army. He did more than serve, of course: he served with devotion, pride and stubbornness. I remembered how he proudly displayed his medals and ribbons. I also remembered visits to concentration camps and encounters with holocaust survivors. How could I reconcile myself to those things? In the same way, how could he have reconciled himself with my decision to change my life so radically without driving himself mad? True, there were times when he discussed the dark side of the Second World War, and in doing so he showed regret. But he was never willing to discuss the horrors and pain inflicted by Germans in the name of Germany.

As I stood there I recalled my mother's role as the always-suffering victim of my father's rage. I also remembered those few rare moments when I witnessed their passionate embrace, but these eventually gave way to the slamming of doors, screams in the night, and tense silence that lasted for days.

But time had passed, and there I was paying tribute to my parents at their final resting place. Torn between regret and sorrow for all I had not done for them and for us, I tried to review for myself why it all happened and why I had responded in the way I did.

What shaped their lives? And how did that shape affect my reality?

Of course it had begun a long time ago, long before I was born, but even after so many years had gone by, I had yet to comprehend what had really happened. What really motivated me to change my life so dramatically? While standing in front of my parent's grave, I wanted to understand their life and mine. My life had come full circle. I had to reach closure here and now.

RUSSIA, OCTOBER 3, 1941

IT WAS A COLD morning, and he awoke drowsy and fatigued. The amphetamine tablets had helped him to stay awake for the three days since the last briefing with the general, but now fatigue finally caught up with him. In the turret of the Tiger tank he felt the cold metal through the thick material of the uniform he had worn for so many days. "Where am I?" was his first thought as he opened his heavy eyelids. His mighty Tiger tank, the pride of the German tank force, rested on top of a hill overlooking the town of Orel, on the Oka River, in western Russia .

As he struggled to clear his mind, he felt the physical and mental strain of the last few months. Since June 22, 1941, the German military forces pushed eastward in their all-out attempt to conquer mighty Russia. With victory now in sight, his tank force had come under the command of the legendary General Guderian, commander of the German Tank Forces, and the conquest of the town below them had taken on great strategic importance. Orel stretched along both banks of the river, only a few hundred miles from Moscow.

The same cold weather facing them had once stopped and defeated the mighty general Napoleon. Days were already getting shorter and colder, and these signs of oncoming winter urged him into action. He had learned as a young boy that taking action for the "Vaterland (Fatherland)" was a definitive sign of courage. He had learned this at the National Political Institutes of Education (NAPOLA), special schools to raise the new leadership of the Nazi regime, where he was also taught that the welfare of the group should be primary the focus of attention and effort.

Fear was a weakness, he learned, and tears were for women. He would be a warrior with an iron heart.

The blood of his ancestors nourished his heart. His grandfather had fought in the war of 1871 against France, and his father sustained serious injuries in the First World War, crawling out of the blood-filled trenches of France. He was the offspring of warriors, an officer of the mighty German Wehrmacht, a young warrior ready and willing to unleash the power of his iron war machine. It was time to act!

As he slowly came to being fully awake he soon realized that he had spent all night in the turret of the Tiger tank. His legs were stiff and his hands nearly frozen. In the early daylight he could survey the position his tank had assumed the night before. He turned his head toward a group of trees on the smooth slope of a hill about 400 yards away. What he saw, nestled among the crown of trees near the bottom of the slope, sent chills down his spine. The powerful 76-mm gun of a Russian T-34 tank was pointing straight at him.

"Oh God," he mumbled in his frozen beard. "They must still be asleep." He pushed at his weapons officer with his right leather boot and a loud gurgle and a curse told him that Heinz was waking up.

"Heinz," he hissed, "get ready for battle. We are going to kill a Russian this morning." He felt the invigorating thrill of the hunt. Every inch of his stiff body was now flooded with adrenalin, sending his blood like hot sparkling wine through his arteries and veins. Today is the day, he thought. Today we will conquer Orel and this is how it will begin. This is my chance to serve Germany.

"Fire," he heard himself scream, tearing apart the frozen skin of his dry lips as he did so. The taste of his own warm blood in his mouth heightened his excitement. Seconds later the explosion of the Russian tank temporarily blinded him as a direct hit ignited the ammunition on board and incinerated everyone within.

At the end of that cold October day the town of Orel surrendered to General Guderian's tank units. Senior Lieutenant Arthur Reinhard Wollschlaeger commanded the first Tiger tank in the attack on the last line of defense around the town.

His prestigious Knight's cross assured, he crossed the bridge over the Oka River. Today Orel, he thought, tomorrow Moscow. Victory for Germany seemed all but assured to the man who would be my father.

RAMALLAH, 1988

THE GRAY ISRAELI ARMY bus rumbled along the road filled with potholes that lead to the army camp. It was early in the morning, and daylight was beginning to light the rolling hills and orchards of olive trees on the slopes above. The bus passed an old Palestinian man standing on the side of the road, smoking a cigarette and wearing a Keffiyah, a traditional headdress of Arab men. He might have been a local farmer, his dried and wrinkled face tightly wrapped around prominent cheekbones. His eyes were dark, staring at us with a mixture of hostility and resignation. He looked straight at me and our eyes met only for a fleeting moment, but long enough to remember that man. I was sitting at one of the windows, which were covered with iron bars, and I felt uneasy in this cage. My new army uniform was covered with a layer of fine dust, which turned my green fatigues to a dirty brown. I clumsily held my M-16, which I had received only the week before, and its cartridge filled with bullets. I was holding it with both hands, trying to keep it pointed at the ceiling of the bus. During countless drills we had been instructed by our sergeant about the use of our rifles, and once we crossed the Green

Line into the West Bank he ordered us to insert the cartridge. The Intifada, or Palestinian uprising, had begun just that month and we were cautioned about stone-throwing teenagers and militant Fatah members who might assault military vehicles.

Despite these looming dangers I felt comfortable in the company of the almost forty other men - new immigrants from all over the world, drafted like me into the Israel Defense Forces. I felt a mixture of tension and relief, almost like a "real" Israeli. After my arrival in Israel, I was assigned to an Immigration Center in a *kibbutz*, or communal settlement, which was based on a unique community concept. It was a socio-economic system based on joint ownership of property, and on equality and cooperation in production, consumption, and education. Initially, most kibbutzim were based on agricultural production, but they soon had to adapt to the changing conditions and integrated manufacturing facilities and even hospitality services.

Several hours daily I had to attend a Hebrew language school, or Ulpan, and there I learned enough modern Hebrew, also called Ivrith, to get along. The remainder of the day I spent working in the banana fields of the kibbutz, which gave me physical strength and endurance.

Still, I felt like I was living in a bubble, protected from the real experience of life in Israel. After receiving my draft orders I knew that the honeymoon was over and I had to face a new chapter of life in my adopted homeland away from home. Here I was, a German and now a soldier in the uniform of the Israel Defense Forces. How did I get there?

It came as a sudden and unwelcome realization: I was a soldier very much like my father. He had fought in the war I despised so much and fought for what I saw as the wrong ideals. Now I was here, serving in the Army of the county founded as a homeland for the same people my father's army had tried to exterminate. But why? What triggered this dramatic change in my life? Born and growing up in postwar Germany, I had been unaware of my father's past. This was far from uncommon.

Nobody spoke about Germany's infamous past. My family most tacitly avoided asking questions. But once I discovered this, I could no longer avoid the questions. From that point on my actions and inactions played an important role in changing my life. Was it guilt that drove me? Or the shame of belonging to a people who still harbored the perpetrators of unspeakable crimes against the people I had now chosen to join?

I knew I had yet to deal with these issues, but had not yet allowed myself to do so – to reflect on the dramatic shift in my life and how it affected my family.

My thoughts were interrupted as the bus suddenly turned onto a small road leading to the entrance of the army base. I looked out through the window and saw the outline of the army camp appearing on top of the hill. Several barracks and tents circled around a water tower and were surrounded by a barbed wire fence. The bus came to an abrupt stop at the gate and the sergeant ordered us to leave the bus.

"Dov," he called me, using my Hebrew name now, "watch the back of the bus and be alert. There may be a sniper waiting for us."

"No problem," I answered in my accented Hebrew. I carefully observed the barren area around the bus. Most of the olive trees had been uprooted after snipers hiding in the olive orchards had attacked a bus like ours a few weeks earlier.

Perhaps those were that old man's olive trees, but what could we do?

We had to remove the trees to protect ourselves.

Despite the early morning heat I felt cold and uncomfortable. This would be my home for the next few months. At least it wasn't as cold as in Russia, where my father fought in the Second World War.

I had a burning desire to explain to him why I was here in Israel, convinced that doing so would begin to build the common understanding that had eluded us when he was alive.

But it was too late for that now.

Still, it's a story I have to tell from then on.

GERMANY, 1966

WHEN I WAS EIGHT years old, twenty years after WWII, I lived with my father and mother in Bamberg, a picturesque town in beautiful Bavaria. It was at this point in my life that my father's work took him far away, disrupting our family life. My father had advanced in his professional career, utilizing the military skills he had acquired during his wartime service. They were once again valued – not for soldiering, but for administrative work with the German Civil Defense Ministry. His job as a senior civil servant was demanding, and he had to live and work in distant Bonn, the nation's capital. He agreed to the move because he was passionate about helping to create a strong civil defense system.

He had experienced the suffering of German civilians first-hand during and after the Second World War, and he supported the new post-war government's emphasis on rebuilding a new German Army to protect the emerging democracy.

Unfortunately, this meant that I saw him only about once a month more seldom than I would have liked. I looked forward to my father's visits. They always began with me waiting outside the house for his car to turn the corner into our small street. I would stand waiting patiently for him to leave the car. He would embrace my mother first, and then me.

When I saw him, I immediately wanted to share everything that happened to me since we last spoke. At eight years of age, there were so many new experiences to talk about: exciting new knowledge I acquired in school, the discoveries I had made with friends, and of course all the different books I had read since his absence. I felt there were so many other things he should know about me. He seemed to enjoy having me talk with him and I considered those moments as my most precious times with him.

Still, we could never completely break through the barrier of formality. I had to address him as "Father" – never as "Dad." Too much of the time he was rather cold and distant. He rarely showed me empathy or warmth, and I always sensed that he was detached and formal. I missed him very much when he was gone. I felt we had too little time to talk.

In retrospect I think that my father must have looked forward to our times together.

He honestly tried to understand and guide me in this rapidly changing world, but the times required more than he was capable of understanding.

When he came home he usually took me on hunting trips in the Bavarian forest.

On these trips he tried to teach me respect for weapons and how to use them properly.

He had experienced the terrible toll that weapons can inflict, and from within his powerful Tiger tank he knowingly killed many people. He had done so legitimately, so he told me, as a soldier following orders, an explanation that he seemed to think was sufficient. He admitted to sadness at having witnessed many comrades torn to pieces by grenades and machinegun fire, and he admitted that their cries for help still pierced his mind. He himself had been wounded five times on battlefields in Poland and Russia, and his last injury was the most serious, an open head wound caused by grenade shrapnel. This wound caused him to suffer recurrent headaches and fainting spells throughout his life, and my mother claimed that it was also responsible for his bouts of uncontrollable anger.

While my father never questioned his own role in the war, he was not altogether pleased by his country's treatment of its warriors. Three of his four brothers were killed in the Second World War, he still called the "Great War," dying for the same fatherland he had served. Nonetheless, their deaths were never formally acknowledged, nor their service publicly appreciated. This perceived insult was part of the pervasive loss of social status a WWII soldier suffered in his defeated homeland. It was compounded by the meager disability payment he received in recognition of his own war injuries, left him a bitter and frustrated man.

Even so, he continued to believe in the warrior's values, and during his monthly visits he would monitor my educational development in that light. He told me that at the age of eight I was old enough to start my "real" education. To him, this meant that I should be raised in the same way he was, adopting such habits as a short military haircut, proper attire, flawless command of the German language, and honor and respect for family and fatherland. A "real" German, he said, should be strong and tough enough to withstand the tide of history that had washed away so many traditions and values.

It pained him deeply that in post-war Germany nobody dared to use the term fatherland and even disdained the national pride he still felt so deeply. The war had devastated Germany, tearing families apart, dividing the nation and leaving it under the control of the allied forces.

Like most Germans, my father believed that a new country had to be rebuilt, but the country was divided in how to pursue that goal. While he believed in honor, strength, and perseverance, these same values were being questioned and even mocked by the young generation whose anger was expressed in the student rebellion of the 1960s.

Anarchism and even terrorism threatened to spread, adding to father's feelings of anger and helplessness.

My father's character was shaped in fundamental ways by my grandfather. Grandfather Reinhardt was born into a Prussian military family, serving with distinction in the First World War, when he lost his right leg and suffered multiple wounds. When he returned home to a defeated Germany, he felt humiliated and confused about the defeat of his proud and mighty nation. How could his beloved Germany have endured the daily death of thousands of young soldiers? How could it have suffered such a crushing defeat?

He could think of only one explanation for the country's situation, which he preached to my father every day. It was that Communists and Social Democrats, most of them of Jewish descent, had sabotaged the efforts of the loyal German troops who fought in the blood-stained trenches and subverted the country itself through a thousand secret plots and betrayals.

As far as I could gather, my grandfather was the family's dominating figure, and his firm beliefs became family truths. He demanded absolute obedience from everyone and tolerated no questioning of his authority or his version of reality. He ordered all his male children – my father and his four brothers – to serve in the Army and allowed them to contemplate no other career path. My father and his brothers dared not question his authority nor deviate from the path laid down for them.

However, my grandfather's early and untimely death deprived my father of his primary role model, confusing and perhaps wounding him so deeply that he refused to even talk with me about him. My grandfather died on a gray winter day in 1930, and several weeks later my grandmother Wilhelmina succumbed to influenza. My father was twelve years old at the time, the youngest of four brothers and four sisters. He was sent away to live with relatives and separated from his siblings. I remember asking him about his brothers and sisters, my uncles and aunts. He was very tightlipped about the subject and reacted angrily when I pressed him about his past.

As he grew into a young man, he adapted his father's version of Germany's sorry plight in the wake of the First World War. This version of the truth included not only the alleged subversive activities of the Jews and the Communists who hatched "secret deals with the enemy" to guarantee their own survival, but also the weakness of the German leaders led by Emperor Wilhelm, who had succumbed to the post-war demands of the allies.

Chief among the crimes of Emperor Wilhelm, in the view of my father and grandfather, was his acceptance of the Treaty of Versailles, which forced Germany to accept sole responsibility for beginning the First World War and imposed an enormous burden of financial retribution on the country crippling its economy for years to come.

For many Germans like my grandfather, this was a time of betrayal and loss at many levels, created by the harsh pressures exerted by the allies. The actual peace negotiations began in Versailles, France, after the ceasefire of November 11, 1918. The negotiations were conducted by the victorious allied forces, but the final conditions were laid down by the "Big Three:" the United States, France, and Great Britain.

Germany itself was excluded from the negotiations, and its foreign minister signed the final treaty on June 28, 1919, under protest. Its harsh terms included the surrender of parts of German territory to France and the forfeiture of its colonies in Africa.

The allied powers also dismantled Germany's military structure to reduce its ability to wage war again.

As a result, my father had no army he could serve in and no war he could fight. He often asked himself why he was he born into such "shallow" and "humiliating" times, when Germany was ruled by politicians lacking aristocratic backgrounds and demeaned by journalists who mocked authority. I imagine my father was an intelligent and ambitious young man who was fascinated by uniforms and marches and who wanted to become a soldier and officer. Unfortunately, for him, Germany's armed forces were but a pale vestige of their former might.

My father grew up hearing and eventually believing that the Treaty of Versailles was stifling not only the growth but also the very existence of his country, and he was eager to find a way to break the perceived chains of oppression. He was taught and believed that Germany must expand to accommodate its growing population.

"We need our Lebensraum – our living space," he heard often, referring to the vast expanse of land to the East. This, people began to say, would be the new frontiers of a mighty Germany.

One of the people saying this most determinedly, of course, was Adolf Hitler, who was just rising to power when my grandfather died in 1930. According to Hitler's race-based ideology, all Germans belonged to the Aryan race whose pure blood contained the soul of the people.

According to this ideology, God had created the Aryans to be the most perfect culture, both physically and spiritually. Their blood-based spiritual energy would fuel the final emergence of German culture as the ultimate expression of a perfected humanity.

To mix and dilute this blood with that of any non-Aryan populations would jeopardize the perfection of Aryan culture. Therefore the proper national strategy would require the removal of all non-Aryans from Germany and the addition of sufficient land to allow the growth of the Aryan population. So Hitler declared in his infamous book "Mein Kampf" which struck a responsive cord in German's who believed it was their destiny to dominate Europe and the World.

Such a vision, of course, held strong appeal for my father. Hitler provided him with a new father figure to replace my grandfather, as well as a practical strategy for reclaiming the former greatness of Germany. He was therefore exhilarated to be sent to a special school (NAPOLA), established to groom Germany's emerging military and political leadership. He thrived under the severe conditions of the academy which enforced rigorous discipline and banned all discussions. Emotions or feelings were considered inferior qualities, unbecoming for a true German, and their expression was not permitted in this breeding ground of Aryan manhood.

The NAPOLA curriculum was geared toward one goal: obedience. German students were expected to become obedient servants of the state, and strict discipline was to be maintained at all times in both the school and home environments. Students learned only what was determined by the Nazi ideology to be "good" for Germany and would support Germany's advancement. If a field of study or a particular view was not approved by the Nazi party, it was "bad" for Germany and not taught. Teachers had to represent the Aryan race and the Nazi party ideology. Any doubt about either quality triggered immediate removal from their teaching position. Students were taught to obey natural rules, beginning with survival of the fittest. The disabled and the weak had no place in the new Germany.

Cruel physical education programs forced the students to exercise outdoors in winter wearing only shorts and to swim in icy water. Any digression from the rules resulted in severe physical punishment and humiliating expulsion. The academy's mandate was to create a new breed of German leaders. My father wanted to be one of this new breed and to lead his own troops to conquer the world. Germany, he thought, is not going to be defeated again.

On January 31, 1933 Adolf Hitler became Germany's new chancellor, promising to restore the nation to a position of power and glory. He would begin by removing all those elements that contributed to Germany's defeat. Few people realized the systemic and deliberate deceit hidden in his promises, and those who did so out loud, quietly and permanently disappeared. My father, like the majority, responded positively to Hitler's vision, eagerly joining the new German army at a time when war was on everyone's mind and lips. He shared the popular view that Germany's might needed to be restored and believed that it was the duty of every loyal and right-minded German to do his part.

Little did he know that this new start for Germany would signify the beginning of its demise. Thirteen years of Hitler's totalitarian rule almost fatally tarnished German's image, destroyed countless lives, and stained the national soul for generations.

When I was growing up, we had contentious debates about my father's own decisions as a young man, while he lamented my generation's absence of national commitment. He could not understand how, as a young German, I could not identify with the ideals he still believed in; nor could I make him see how those ideals were discredited by the blood of millions of Nazi Germany's victims.

WHEN MY FATHER WAS away in Bonn, I could never escape my mother's desire to protect me from outside influences. She was always afraid that something might happen to me, and that I might not succeed in life.

This prevented me from seeking a deep emotional connection with her. Our relationship was not based on trust, but on respect. I do not doubt that she loved me, but her overprotective attitude almost smothered me. In retrospect, I realized that her smothering was driven by her fear of losing me, like so many things that she had already lost.

Her inability to let me grow up and to lovingly allow myself to separate from her forced me to cut the umbilical cord before I was strangled.

One day I had failed to follow a teacher's instructions. This particular teacher was a relic of the authoritarian education system of the pre-war regime. He enforced absolute obedience with a whip. That day we were supposed to complete a homework assignment that included carefully cutting out monopoly money currency printed on thick paper sheets. The resulting paper coins and bills were to be used to teach us to count money. We were told to cut along the lines, but I did not follow orders. I presented him my homework which consisted of ripped and torn monopoly money. My teacher yelled at me and demanded an explanation. I remember that I refused to answer and just smiled in defiance. He was so angry he whipped my face, hands, and buttocks until I bled.

When my mother picked me up from school, my face was so swollen that she began to cry.

"What did you do wrong?" she screamed. "Why do you never listen to the teacher?" She didn't gave me a chance to explain, but confined me to my room. I could not understand why she had not even asked what happened, or why she was so quick to side against me.

My mother, my only refuge and shelter during my father's absence, had turned against me, not even attempting to understand me. She uncritically supported the teacher's actions because he represented authority, and she was terrified of disobeying authority, even if it meant she had to witness the suffering of her own child. This event deeply fractured the bond between. I could no longer trust her. I stayed awake at night, crying and feeling alone and abandoned.

I was further confused when I saw my father and mother express great affection for each other. When he came for visits, he would immediately embrace, kiss, and hug her as I stood by. I felt happy for both of them, but it seemed odd that both never expressed themselves this way with me. In addition, my mother's fears ended up coming between me and my father. Inevitably he would ask how I was doing in school.

Hearing my mother's long list of complaints and criticisms, I knew that I was going to receive several lashes from his belt after those from my teacher. My father was unable to articulate his anger and frustration with me. He considered physical punishment the only way to express his feelings. He could not verbalize his anger and displeasure. He was either constitutionally incapable, unable, or unwilling to do so, and I silently suffered my beatings.

Thankfully, I could always escape into the imaginary world described in my books.

I loved reading all types of books, especially those about explorers seeking unknown horizons and great new opportunities. I wished I could escape and travel like Marco Polo or Columbus. I knew there was more in the world to explore than I might ever imagine. I dreamed that I would have the opportunity to travel and visit faraway places. I also knew that one day I would live out that dream.

THE MYSTERY OF THE LADY UPSTAIRS

OUR HOUSE WAS AN old gray two-story stone and brick building that belonged to a noble family. We had to walk up steps to the main entrance, which led into a small entry hall that was divided by a stairway leading to the upstairs apartment. We lived on the first floor and the landlady lived above us. A large painting of a proud-looking uniformed man towered over the stairway. As a young boy I always wondered about that man, who looked handsome in his uniform of a high-ranking officer. But when I asked my father about him he angrily refused to talk about him.

"Never ask about this man," he said in a gruff tone. "He was a traitor, and his family should be ashamed of him."

Of course this reaction baffled me, and only sharpened my appetite to solve this mystery. Why did my father despise the proud-looking man who once wore the same uniform my father did?

As long as my father was home, I was forbidden from visiting the apartment upstairs, but I found it difficult to resist the urge when the opportunity arose. One rainy day I was sitting in my room with nothing to do, so I did some exploring. When my mother was busy ironing I snuck out of the apartment, walked up the stairs, and knocked on the door. After a few anxious moments, a woman opened the door and regarded me with a stern expression.

"How can I help you Bernd?"

I was surprised that she knew my name. I had seen her before and knew that she lived here, but my parents had never introduced us. For her part, she had never said a word to me as we passed on the stairs. Our eyes would meet only for seconds, but she never smiled or winked.

"Did your father allow you to come up here? As far as I know he is not very fond of me and I am quite sure he would not like you to be here." I was intimidated by her stern voice and serious expression, but her eyes were warm maybe even a bit sad.

"I am bored and want to play," I answered. "Can I stay here a little while? My mother is busy and I don't want to play alone."

She hesitated, then let me into her apartment. I walked into a huge room decorated with antique furniture and more pictures of the man in the portrait downstairs.

She asked me to sit down, and after a long silence I summoned up my courage.

"Who is the man in the picture?" I asked. She paused and closed her eyes for a moment, but quickly regained her composure and looked at me with a slight smile.

"That is my husband. He was a handsome and proud man. His name was Claus von Stauffenberg and I was his wife Nina." She sighed as she said their names.

I was full of questions.

"Where is he now? I have never seen him in this house. Does he still live here?"

"No," she answered, "he is long gone and does not live here anymore." Her eyes now filled with tears and her voice broke. Again she summoned up her composure and spoke briskly.

"That's enough. You have to leave now."

I didn't understand what I had done to upset her, and it was only later that I learned more about the man my father called a traitor and whom I learned to respect as a hero.

Claus Philipp Maria Count Schenk von Stauffenberg was a German army officer who fought during the Second World War in Africa, where he lost an eye and an arm in military action. He returned to Germany, and after recovering from his injuries, he was made chief-of-staff to General Fromm at the Reserve Army headquarters. In this position he belonged to the select few who attended Hitler's military conferences where he had close, regular access to Hitler himself. Little is known about his personal motivation, but his education and upbringing seemed to have shaped his personal and religious views. He considered Hitler a threat to the survival of the German nation and decided to come to Germany's rescue. On July 20, 1944, he played a pivotal role in the assassination attempt against Hitler.

Von Stauffenberg was not alone in his conviction. Several previous attempts by young officers to assassinate Hitler were either foiled by the secret police or never materialized. Those attempts were triggered by the growing discontent among Hitler's officers about the war. Others allege that the rumors of mass murders in concentration camps may also have contributed to their decision to remove Hitler from power.

Even though those reports could not be verified by the officers themselves, they were sufficiently credible that young officers were willing to risk their lives in order to stop Hitler.

By the time von Stauffenberg acted, Hitler had grown increasingly suspicious and avoided contact with any military officers but those screened by his secret service. Nonetheless, on July 20 1944, during one of the military conferences, von Stauffenberg succeeded in placing a briefcase bomb under the table around which Hitler and more than twenty officers had gathered. When he left the room about ten minutes later, he was convinced that the bomb would kill the dictator. The bomb did explode, but the blast was muffled by the heavy oak table. Three officers were killed, but Hitler survived with minor injuries. Von Stauffenberg returned to Berlin to join the other officers involved in the planning and execution of the assassination plot, unaware that Hitler had survived. They were beginning the steps intended to take control of the government and call for immediate peace negotiations with the allied forces when he and his comrades were arrested. Count von Stauffenberg and several of his comrades were executed in the early morning hours of the very next day. On Hitler's personal orders his pregnant wife Nina was sent to a prison camp; their other four children were kept in an orphanage under false names until the end of the war. After Germany's defeat she was liberated by the allied forces from a prison, reunited with her children, and settled in Bamberg in the building owned by her husband's family. It was there that I grew up.

As a boy I could not understand why my father would live in the building owned by the family of the man he regarded as a traitor. My mother later revealed to me that he had little choice. After the war my father was imprisoned by the American army, and after his release he was unable to find employment. As a former army officer he was considered politically unreliable and prevented from accepting any job controlled by the occupying allied forces, which included most available jobs. He never admitted to me that he worked as a door-to-door salesman, and could barely support a family.

During that hard time my mother was desperately seeking housing for the family and was referred to Count Stauffenberg's widow. Recognizing my mother's desperation, she agreed to rent her the large ground-floor apartment. My father grudgingly agreed to accept, but only because he had nowhere else to turn. He tried to ignore the fact that his family was granted refuge in the house belonging to the man he considered a traitor.

I never forgot the image of the man in the painting. After reading about what he had done I tried to understand my father's attitude toward him, but I found that I did not share it.

I realize now that the break between us and his view of history had begun way back then.

Apparently my father refused to accept the truth about why von Stauffenberg tried to assassinate Hitler – to save his beloved Germany from an immoral tyrant. My father believed that discipline, duty and honor superseded personal ethics, moral behavior and responsibility – a belief shared neither by me nor by von Stauffenberg. My father was unable or perhaps unwilling to recognize that a German officer might violate his conscience by blindly following orders with disregard for the ultimate good. He could have refused orders that were immoral or unethical, but he chose not to question his orders, nor did he question orders to murder innocent civilians.

To this day I am unsure whether I wish he had chosen differently. Had he done so, he might have paid for it with his life, just as Count von Stauffenberg did. But wasn't the price worth it when the stakes were so high? Was it not essential to take a stand for your beliefs, no matter what the cost? Or was I expecting too much of my father?

Perhaps he had been so indoctrinated to obey orders – by his grandfather, by NAPOLA, and by his culture – that to do otherwise was for him virtually impossible.

Clearly, his education and schooling omitted the teachings of ethic and moral behavior, but I still wish he had given me his thoughts and feelings about his actions. He either did not dare to question, or was incapable doing so, and I don't know which. I wish he had told me why he considered Stauffenberg's actions treacherous. Did he know about the large-scale murder of Jews, gypsies, homosexuals, the mentally and physically disabled? If he knew, why did he still feel compelled to follow orders given by those committing the murders? My father left me with more questions than answers, and until today I am still trying to sort out these matters.

THE STAR

BAMBERG, THE BEAUTIFUL CITY on the river Main
where I grew up, is so predominantly Catholic that it is sometimes
called the "Rome of the North." In fact, for a short time during the
11th century the city was actually the center of the so-called Holy
Roman Empire. Like Rome, Bamberg was built on seven hills, each
crowned by a church; the main Cathedral marked the city center.
Almost everyone living there is Catholic.

I was baptized Catholic myself and later received my holy
communion there.

As a child I never witnessed the practice of any other religion. I
read about them in books, but I had never actually met a Jew, Muslim
or Buddhist. But as I grew older, my general thirst for knowledge
included a yearning to know more about all other cultures and
religions.

Although my father was raised as a Protestant, he never practiced
his faith and discouraged us from attending any formal religious
services. My mother disagreed with him on that issue, attending
church on Sundays and taking me with her, but those experiences
never instilled religious feelings in me.

When I was nine years old I had my first glimpse of the importance
of religion when my mother took me to see a dentist in the center
of the city. At a two-story white apartment building, we rang the bell;
the exterior door opened and we climbed a stairway leading into a
small hallway.

There was a door on the ground level that was covered with
colorful glass.

I noticed a large golden star above the doorway. I found it simple
and beautiful – two intertwined triangles forming a hexagram. I had
never seen such a symbol before and asked my mother what it was.
She had already seen the star, turned her eyes away, and appeared
to be startled and even frighten by it. Clutching my hand, she pulled
me upstairs to the dentist's office without answering my question or
saying a word.

She remained silent for most of that day, and when I asked what
was troubling her, she turned to me with tears in her eyes, grasping

my shoulders.

"Do not come too close to that star," she said. "You will only suffer. We all suffered so much during the war and we need to put that behind us now."

Of course I didn't understand a word of this, or why she so afraid, and she would not explain. Did the symbol remind her of the yellow star, inscribed with the word "Jew," which was the symbol of Nazi persecution? If she was a Catholic, why was she afraid of persecution?

One day my older sister told me something equally strange.

"If you shake our family tree," she said, "a Jew will fall to the ground." She never explained what that meant, but my mother's fearful reaction must have had some basis. I never found out if our family tree included any Jewish limbs, but in retrospect I wondered why the eyes and hair of our family was darker than the average German. Whenever I mentioned that fact, my mother would quickly explain that we were of Southern descent, but would go no further.

I never forgot that star and was wondering what it was all about. I suspected that it carried great significance for me. At future visits my mother would take me only as far as the front door, never coming inside. I did not mind because it gave me the opportunity to admire the star for a moment as I passed, and inspired me to learn more about the symbol. Little did I know that many years later I would not only return to this building, but enter by the front door to visit the home of the tiny Jewish community center that gathered behind the glass door I had passed on my earlier visits to the dentist.

MOVING TO BONN: CONTINUING THE SEARCH FOR MY PAST

SOMETIME AROUND MY TENTH birthday, my father announced that our family would finally be reunited. He had received a promotion to senior administrator in the German Civil Defense Ministry in Bonn, still the German capital, and I was happy to hear that we could join him there. I was also ready to escape the confines of the old city of Bamberg and to experience more of the world.

We settled in Meckenheim, a small suburb of Bonn where I was enrolled in the local middle school. I found it difficult to fit in because of my southern dialect, which was ridiculed by my peers. So I often sought refuge in the local library where I was comforted by the many walls of books. I not only sought answers to my endless questions about the world, but the world of books also allowed me to disconnect from the world I was living in putting me more at ease. I did not know which world I wanted to escape more badly – my father's static and rigid view of the world, or the unfriendly environment of Meckenheim – but my reading removed me from both.

At the same time, my knowledge grew rapidly, of course, and my teachers realized that I was a strong candidate for a university degree. I was eventually transferred to a gymnasium, a secondary school that prepared students for university education, where I fit well into the system of higher learning. My favorite subjects were languages, humanities, and biology.

To that list I soon added history and politics because my father had encouraged me to read newspapers and magazines from an early age. Naturally, he selected conservative publications for me, but he could not suppress my interest in other newspapers I found in the library. Those publications quickly showed me how limited and outdated was my father's worldview.

We also had a small but impressive library of books at home, which included a large though outdated encyclopedia that opened a window for me on the histories of the Greek and Roman Empires, Asia, Europe, and North America. Of course I never found any relevant information on the period of recent German history in which my father had participated.

My father continued to offer only silence about that period, except to describe his military training before the war and of course his participation in the capture of Orel, which he told me so many times I almost came to believe I had been there myself.

He repeatedly described how he approached the city at the head of a column of tanks, the excitement he felt when he destroyed a Russian tank, and the thrilling military honor bestowed upon him by Adolf Hitler himself, who personally attached the Knight's cross to his uniform.

For all the times I listened patiently these stories, he never encouraged or even allowed me to ask any questions. I asked repeatedly about his mother, my other grandparents, my five uncles and four aunts, but he avoided talking about them. On one occasion, for example, when I asked a direct question about that period in Germany's history, his expression hardened and he looked at me with cold eyes.

"Son," he said, "I have told you everything you need to know." In his view, I suppose, he was right, but this meant carefully avoiding discussion of anybody in his family except his father, and included only his father's military career and service during World War One. I knew from his grim expression that further questioning would lead not to answers but to a beating, so I dropped the subject once again. I was not satisfied, of course, and awaited my next chance to seek answers

I continually wondered why my father kept silent about so many parts of his life, and it was not until much later that I came to the conclusion that facing the past would trigger emotions he was afraid to release and would not be able to control. Certainly having dedicated his life to the service of Germany conflicted with the feeling that the fatherland had betrayed him. He tried serving honorably as an officer, but this was impossible to reconcile with the horrific crimes committed in the name of his beloved Germany. I believe he wanted to forget and move on, but the past never allowed him to do so.

My mother, on the other hand, although I chafed under her need to "protect" me from the world, was at least forthcoming when I questioned her about her own life before the war. She was born in Karlsbad, a picturesque town located in the Sudeten mountain region along the border of Bohemia, Moravia and Silesia, or present-day Slovakia. The ethnic Germans in this region were called Sudeten Germans, descendants of Medieval German colonists invited by the Kings of Bohemia into these previously Slavic areas for agricultural cultivation. The area was captured by Germany in 1938 and is now part of the Czech Republic. Karlsbad is known for its medicinal springs which attracted European aristocrats and dignitaries to the region.

My mother came from a wealthy family of business people and, as best I can remember, her father owned a factory that manufactured fine leather gloves. My mother lived a sheltered life with loving and overprotective parents who kept her safe from the deteriorating political conditions around her. She described in detail the large villa she grew up in; her dog, a St.Bernard named Alto; and her parrot, Lora. Her description of her life reminded me of a princess living in a remote castle in fairyland – a world of loving, caring people that would never change. That soon proved to be untrue, of course, as the world around her changed suddenly and the political turmoil disrupted her life as it did so for many others.

The Germans were the largest ethnic group in this border region of Germany, Austria and Czechoslovakia, and their presence had always provoked controversy with the Czechs. With the rise of Nazism the conflict was aggravated by local followers of the emerging Nazi party, which was led by the local agitator Konrad Henlein. Under his leadership, the German-speaking ethnic majority demanded more autonomy. Adolf Hitler was eager to be the spokesperson for their demands, although they had no understanding that they were just one pawn in his greater aspirations. In 1938 Hitler claimed that the Sudeten Germans in Czechoslovakia were being abused and oppressed by the Czech government, and demanded the "return" of the region to Nazi Germany.

Naturally the Czech government refused, and the matter was arbitrated by the Western nations. To appease Hitler, England, France, and Italy pressured the Czech government to cede the disputed territories to Germany, and on September 30th, 1938, representatives of those countries signed the Munich Agreement ceding the Sudetenland to Germany.

The Czechoslovak government was forced to abide by the agreement, and in October the Sudetenland was occupied by Germany. This "unification" with Nazi Germany, now also called the "Third Reich," was followed by the expulsion of the Czech population to other parts of Czechoslovakia, which in March 1939 were invaded and occupied by Germany.

By chance, my father was one of the first German officers to enter the "liberated" Sudeten region, and by yet another chance, my mother was one of the first local people he met.

She always repeated telling me the same story about that fateful day when she met my father. One day in April 1939 a German officer knocked at the door of my grandfather's house, and it was my mother, then a woman in her early twenties, who opened the door and faced a tall, handsome man in a German uniform.

"Good morning," he said to her politely, "I am sorry to disturb you, my name is Lieutenant Arthur Wollschlaeger, and I am seeking your parent's permission to stay in your house."

The Sudeten Germans were expected to host German officers in their houses, and this was one of many such encounters between military officers and civilians. But for my mother, and for me, the meeting was as important as life itself. My mother described the moment as love at first sight, as she was virtually swept off her feet by this charming and young officer.

She talked about it all her life, until Alzheimer's disease gradually robbed her of this romantic memory.

Several months later my parents were married in Karlsbad, but their married life was interrupted by Hitler's decision to invade Poland on September 1, 1939. My father was a young tank commander and was one of the first to lead the invasion. The next year, in May of 1940, he also participated in the invasion of Holland and France. He never talked about either adventure, however, simply repeating that he was a faithful soldier who followed orders.

He did tell me more than once, however, that he never joined the Nazi party, but he failed to explain what prevented him from doing so.

My mother said she pressured him to stay away from politics and to focus on his military career, which did not require Nazi party membership.

He was a bit more forthcoming about his military experience. More than once he expressed his utter contempt for the SS units [Schutzstaffel, or Defense Squadron] that followed the regular army units, "cleaning up the mess," as he called it. He seemed to have knowledge of the methods used by the SS units, but he refused to talk about what he knew. Of course his evasive behavior and angry responses to my questions only heightened my suspicions. What

did he really do? What did he really know? What happened in the
territories he helped to "conquer?" The only first-hand information
he ever shared with me was his story of the attack on the Russian
city of Orel, which he proudly told me over and over, along with
how he was awarded the Knight's cross by Adolf Hitler himself, on
January 12, 1942. The Knight's cross symbolized the recognition of
supreme battlefield bravery and service for his beloved fatherland,
and he considered this award to be the ultimate achievement of his
entire life. The military symbol itself originated in Prussia and was
awarded by Prussia and then Germany to heroic officers and soldiers
during the Franco-Prussian War, the First World War, and the Second
World War. The Nazi regime added a swastika to the center of the
Knight's cross, so that after the war he was not allowed to wear it in
public – unless he removed the swastika. I was forced to endure the
sight of it each Christmas, when my father, in his finest suit, would
wear the Knight's cross around his neck as he led the choir in festive
hymn-singing. I instinctively felt intimidated by the dark silver cross,
despite the pride he obviously experienced. It seemed to separate
us, and to separate the past from the present and the future. As a
young boy I adored my father as a war hero, but gradually the aura
of his heroic deeds was overshadowed by his omissions and silences
about everything else. Suspecting that he was concealing events he
did not want me to know about, I did not want to be identified with
that shadowy past or the Knight's cross that seemed only to widen the
distance between us.

My father's military career ended abruptly when he sustained
the serious head wound I have mentioned. He was transported to
a German military hospital, and while he was treated there, the US
Third Army liberated Karlsbad, on May 5th, 1945, and my mother
and her parents were forced to abandon their belongings and flee
their home.

My mother remained traumatized by those events until the end of
her life. She repeatedly retold the story of how she and her parents
had to sneak along small country roads at night, hiding in forests
during the day, to avoid marauding bands of Russian troops.

I was born on May 9, 1958, almost exactly thirteen years after
the end of the war. My parents had still not recovered from the

war-induced traumas they had each suffered. I suspect that as a result they were actively trying to shield me from anything remotely connected to the events of their past. During the formative years of my childhood and early adolescence, therefore, I received only scanty, filtered information about their families' history, my father's participation in the war, and my mother's terrifying escape from her home.

I tried piecing together information on my own to shed light on their real life. For me my parents were pretending to live "normal" lives, not unlike many other Germans who were desperately trying to forget and to move on. Afraid of expressing their fears and emotions, their faces seemed like wax masks when any war-related topic came up.

All their emotion were suppressed: I never saw my father or mother cry; I never experienced a warm fatherly embrace; we co-existed at a formal distance.

For me, parts of their personalities seemed to be vacant as they "moved on with their lives." They were always moving forward, never looking back. The absence of an emotional relationship with my parents deeply affected my development as a human being. While my mother literally overfed me in her concern for my physical well-being, satiety could not compensate for my hunger for emotional and spiritual nourishment.

I especially missed contact with other family members. My friends all had uncles, aunts, and grandparents, but I seemed to have no living relative. I continually felt their absence.

I remember in particular one Friday night in winter I spent with my parents at home. It had been a cold and sunless day and the world was gray and colorless. In silence my father read the paper and my mother knitted.

"Mother, why don't I have any uncles, "I asked.

My father pretended not to have heard, but his face revealed his anger. My mother sensed the instant tension and chose to ignore my question.

"Just keep playing with your toy cars," she said curtly.

"Now is not the time to talk about it."

I turned toward the window where the outside seemed darker and more menacing. Nobody would shed light on the past.

I knew only that my paternal grandparents had died long before the war, and my mother's parents had died as refugees in post-war Germany, but I could not pry any more information about our family history from my parents whose mission was to conceal and forget.

At times I witnessed my mother gently reminding my father to contact his surviving brother and sister, but his reaction was always one of anger.

When I asked who and where these relatives were, I was rebuffed.

In the absence of any real relatives, my parents made the bizarre request that I call some of their close friends "uncles" and "aunts." Knowing that they were not my real relatives made me even more curious. Even as a child I wondered what had changed my parents' lives so dramatically and how those horrific events would influence my own life.

OLD COMRADES

LATE ONE EVENING IN 1967, when I was nine years old, I was awakened by loud singing and noisy conversation. My father's old army friends, he called them "old comrades", often met at our house for a long night of eating, drinking and intense discussions lasting into the wee hours of the morning. At nine years of age I was somewhat frightened at the prospect of facing those drunken men in our living room. They were my father's "old friends from the war," I was told. That was all.

One of those parties got so loud that I hid in the corner of my room, trying not to hear, but I was assaulted by that same song over and over, one sentence repeating like a broken record: "Deutschland, Deutschland ueber alles - Germany, Germany above all other lands," followed by a single loud, hoarse, and drunken voice singing "D*ie Fahne Hoch* - The flag on high." This song in particular scared me even without knowing its origin, and its roaring melody frightened me all the more when I later learned about it. The song was the anthem of the Nazi Party chosen to honor a Nazi activist named Horst Wessel, who was murdered by a Communist in 1930 and later glorified as a Nazi martyr. This song was and is banned by law in post-war Germany, and I heard my mother's worried voice begging my father's old comrades to stop singing it, but they acted as if she wasn't even there. Meanwhile, up in my room, I was trembling with fear.

I pretended I had not heard my father's friends howling and hoped that my father wouldn't join them singing this terrifying song. I still idealized him and yearned for him to come to my room, caress my head, kiss me on the forehead, and wish me a good night. But this never happened. Only my mother did so, but not consistently. I wanted to run down the stairs to help my mother stop the singing, but I did not have the courage to face that pack of wolves.

Those evenings were often followed by days of tense silence in our home, due both to my father's hangover and my mother's refusal to talk about it. I knew something bad had happened but did not understand what it was. Nor could I get those terrifying melodies out of my mind, though I did not know what they meant. But I knew they were wrong. I needed to know more about all this. I needed to understand.

MUNICH 1972

ON AUGUST 26, 1972, I was glued to our new black and white television set, watching the opening ceremony of the first Olympic Games to take place in Germany since the end of the Second World War. I was watching the athletes march into the new Olympic stadium in Munich when I noticed the same star I had seen years before near the dentist's office. Now it appeared on a flag held high by a smiling man leading the Israeli Olympic team.

I was struck again by its simplicity, and felt that it emanated perfection and strength.

This symbol seemed overwhelming to me, and seemed unlike anything I had ever seen. Or did it remind me of something I had seen before I ? All I knew was that the star was real. It belonged to someone or something important, but I did not know anything else. Its importance was reinforced when my father and mother, who were watching it with me, both fell silent. I felt tension build in the room and instantly knew, from long experience, not to ask questions. As always, I needed to know why.

On September 5th, 1972, the Olympic celebrations came to a horrifying halt when, in the early morning, eight Palestinian terrorists broke into the Olympic Village, killed two members of the Israeli team, and took nine more hostage. Even my father was shocked, though not for the same reasons I was.

He kept repeating,

"How can anyone dare to interrupt these games? These are our games and it's our time now to show the world that Germany is back on the world stage. We are again somebody and those bastards are smearing our image."

Despite his indignation, the interruption continued to unfold, progressing from bad to worse as we watched spellbound. On live television we saw a hooded terrorist peeking out from the balcony of an apartment at the Olympic village. A man in a white suit and hat with dark sunglasses talked with German negotiators. I felt certain something bad was going to happen, and it did. In a botched attempt by the German police to free the hostages, all nine were murdered during a gun battle at the small military airport at Fuerstenfeldbruck. The airport was not far from Dachau, the former concentration camp, where one of my uncles almost lost his life.

The next day a memorial service was held at the Olympic stadium, but it was boycotted by all Arab delegations. During the ceremony German President Gustav Heinemann delivered a speech, showing callous disregard of the innocent lives lost as he decreed that "the games must go on." How dared they continue the games after such an unspeakable crime? The bodies of the killed Israel athletes were returned to Israel for a funeral, which was also televised. I saw the now-familiar star on a flag draped over each coffin and heard a strange prayer in a language I never heard. I later learned the importance of this prayer and its name, Kaddish. Without knowing its meaning I felt its deep importance and tears came to my eyes as I listened. I also experienced the power of the star, as those athletes took it with them to their graves.

The next day at school I heard for the first time the word "Jew" and "Israel" from our social studies teacher. He was in his late forties, and had grown up in Nazi Germany and experienced its downfall.

He was visibly uncomfortable with the words for "Jew" and "Jewish," obviously thinking that we would react strongly to them, but most of us were indifferent because we had neither met a Jew nor learned what one was.

I could not help asking my question.

"What is so special about Jews that makes them the target of such attacks?"

My teacher took a deep breath before responding.

"Because some people believe that they are special and too powerful, and in my opinion they are," he said.

I persisted.

"But they were only trying to compete in the Olympics, and I don't see that as being special."

"Well, there are things that happened in the past," he said.

"Horrible crimes leading to the death of millions of them. The State of Israel was formed to offer them some sort of reprieve. But that led to the expulsion of another people called Palestinians and to war with the Arab countries breeding despair and hatred. The attacks and murderous acts yesterday are just a part of the struggle taking place in the Middle East."

Still I kept after him.

"But the Olympics are supposed to represent peaceful competition between different nations."

His voice was trembling now.

"I know. I thought so too, and I never imagined that that could happen again on German soil. After all that was done against the Jews in the name of Germany."

At that time I had already learned some facts about the killing of Jews during the war, but in our history books the murder of Jews was depicted as casualties of war.

"But shouldn't it be our responsibility to voice our concerns and outrage about this crime committed against the Israelis?" I asked.

He had regained his composure and now was speaking in a calm and commanding voice.

"In some way they have brought it upon themselves. This attack was just another skirmish in the Israeli-Palestinian conflict. They are at war and even the Olympics cannot protect them from that and we cannot get involved."

I was shocked by his attitude and also about the silence of my classmates who acquiesced to his opinion. Unfortunately, this opinion was typical of the generation he represented. Born and raised during the war, he had experienced first-hand the near-total destruction of Germany and its struggle to regain international standing. He attended university during the tumultuous days of the student revolt when left-wing German youths rebelled against everything that traditionalists held dear: the conservative government, the rearmament of the German military, the perpetuation of authoritarian thinking in German politics, the admission of former Nazis into the government. Many were especially incensed about the election of Chancellor Kurt Georg Kiesinger in 1966.

He had joined the Nazi party in 1933 and worked at the foreign ministry's radio propaganda department, actively contributing to the distribution of racist Nazi propaganda.

The protest against the political establishment soon turned violent and fueled the formation in 1970 of a small, radical counter-group called the Bader-Meinhof gang.

It named itself the Red Army Faction and launched a form of an urban warfare that resulted in the killing of several prominent German politicians and industrialists. The leaders of this terror group considered themselves part of the worldwide struggle to liberate oppressed people. They joined forces with the Palestinian Liberation Organization (PLO). Gang members were trained in the use of explosives and weapons in Palestinian camps in Lebanon and helped in the war of terror against Israel.

The large number of Red Army sympathizers spread their anti-Israeli propaganda in Germany, but emphasized that their fight was directed not against all Jews, but just against Zionists. Ulrike Meinhoff, one of the founders and leaders of the group, released a widely quoted statement that denied the responsibility of her generation for the Holocaust and glorified the "liberation" campaign of the PLO against Jewish and Israeli targets worldwide.

My teacher certainly seemed to have been influenced by this propaganda, and even though he condemned the murders in Munich, he considered them an extension of the "justified resistance" against the "Israeli occupation regime."

I was frustrated by his attitude and the fact that the games went on, but I could do nothing. In my view, the athletes who were carrying the flag with the star so proudly were killed by a gang of assassins. What was it about the star that triggered such powerful emotions, magically attracting me but repelling others, including my parents. I had no way of knowing how important that star would become for me, for the rest of my life.

I soon learned that the star originated in the land of Israel, which seemed to be a land of joyful faces and strong men who raised their national flag in pride. It was also a land that buried its fallen heroes in that same flag. I wanted to learn more.

I needed to go there.

Since I was only fourteen at the time and lacked the resources to make such a visit, I had to content myself with reading every book I could find in the public library about Israel. As I did so, I often caught myself daydreaming about this fascinating land.

YOM KIPPUR, 1973

ON OCTOBER 6, 1973, I woke early to take the bus to my job picking apples. I was on fall break and I needed to earn money to feed my habit of buying newspapers, magazines, and books. Mostly I read about Israel. I learned about the history of the Jewish people, their struggle to achieve independence and statehood, biblical archeology, and the geography of the Middle East. I had exhausted the resources of our public library but remained hungry for more. I was passing a newspaper kiosk where a crowd had gathered around the television.

"WHAT HAPPENED?" I ASKED a middle-aged man.

"The Jews are being attacked by the Arabs and I guess this time they will get those bastards," he replied, his eyes dark and cold.

"It's about time somebody took care of them," another man agreed.

Both of them eyed me suspiciously, and one asked,

"Why are you looking at us like that? Are you a Jew lover?" I remained silent and tried to show no expression. These men reminded me of my father's drinking friends who sang "Deutschland, Deutschland, ueber alles."

Not all Germans were like that, but most refused to discuss issues related to the war and the murder of Jews. They wanted to avoid any discussions that might open old wounds. They wanted to remove the years of German history between 1933 and 1945 as a surgeon wants to excise a tumor. But this tumor had metastasized throughout the body and required radical therapy to prevent certain death. Germans had tried to excise the tumor with their silence, but they refused to recognize that the old behavior patterns and stereotypes persisted throughout German culture and society.

On the kiosk television I saw tanks rolling along dusty roads, some of them flying the Israeli flag with the star in the center. The soldiers sitting on the tanks looked stern and I knew the situation was serious.

I did not realize it at the time, but it was Yom Kippur, the "Day of Atonement" and the holiest day of Jewish life and religion. Most Israelis spend the day in the synagogue praying and asking for the forgiveness of their sins. The Arab leaders had chosen this day to attack Israel on all fronts.

I left the television screen and hurried to work, but my mind was preoccupied with the events in Israel. At home I listened to the radio every night that week and witnessed the unfolding of events. On the Golan Heights, approximately two hundred Israeli tanks faced an onslaught of over one thousand Syrian tanks. Along the Suez Canal, fewer than five hundred Israeli defenders were attacked by some eighty thousand Egyptians. At least nine Arab states, including Algeria, Morocco, Sudan, and Tunisia, were actively aiding the Egyptian-Syrian war effort. The Soviet Union supplied the Arab armies with an endless stream of weapons and the United States only belatedly began its own airlift to Israel.

During the first two days of the onslaught, Israel was able to hold off further intrusion of the Arab armies. After mobilizing its reserves, the Israelis pushed the invaders back and carried the war deep into Syria and Egypt. Two weeks after the invasion, Egypt and Syria, the main agents of the attack, were saved from a disastrous defeat by the United Nations Security Council, whose members called a cease-fire, ignoring the responsibility of the Arab countries in initiating the war.

The end of the war was followed by an endless number of funerals for fallen soldiers, and I wondered if the flag with the star would ever again fly proudly in the wind, or would they all be needed to drape the coffins of fallen heroes.

Of course my father noted my obsession with the fate of the Jewish state. Our conversations grew shorter and more aggressive over the next few months, mainly because I could not tolerate his drunken outbursts, his intolerance toward the Jews, and his dismissive behavior toward me. My mother tried to mediate, but she suffered the same treatment and, unlike me, had no avenue of escape.

On that Yom Kippur, he asked me at the dinner table,

"What's new with your Jews? I heard that they are in trouble."

I tried to keep silent, knowing that any answer would invite trouble.

"Answer me!" he demanded.

I raised my head and for the first time I dared to speak to him directly and without fear.

"They have suffered enough and deserve our help."

My mother reacted first.

"Why are you so preoccupied about their suffering? Jews were not the only ones who died in the war. Have you forgotten what I told you about our suffering? We lost everything and had to start all over. We had nothing to do with it and we did not hurt anybody!"

Before I could reply she burst into tears, stood, and left the dinner table. My father stared at me and told me to leave the room. I felt defeated, but knew I was right and promised never to allow myself to get drawn into a conversation about this topic with my parents again. My parents' attempt to compare their suffering during and after the war with that of the Jewish people disgusted me. I knew that ethnic Germans were expelled from their homes in eastern Europe, but there was no master plan to create a network of death camps with the sole purpose of slaughtering millions of innocent victims. I was also aware that thousands of Germans lost their lives during the allied bombing campaign, but the same German people supported their adored leader Adolf Hitler in his war of aggression against the world. My parents represented a generation that refused to comprehend or recognize the extent of the systematic mass murders of the Jewish people, gypsies, and other minorities for no other reason than being stigmatized as "inferior races" who were "cleansed" to make room for the "superior" Aryan race.

THE DARKNESS

MY MOTHER'S EMOTIONAL OUTBURST reflected something terrible that had happened in her lifetime to the Jews she tried to deny or forget. This "something" was never mentioned at school, but I read about it on my own: the millions of Jews who were killed during the war. The systematic killing of almost one-third of the world's entire Jewish population was treated as just another war statistic and all but ignored. The names of the concentration camps – Auschwitz, Birkenau, Bergen Belsen – already rang in my ears, but I had yet to grasp the immensity or the context of the suffering inflicted on the Jewish people.

Nobody in my school, at home, or among my friends spoke of the systematic elimination of the Jewish people from Germany and all territories occupied by the German forces. Nobody was willing to tell me what happened. Many books I found in the library about Jewish history described the glorious and rich culture, but no book talked about the pain and suffering inflicted on Jews by my people. It was a subject ignored. I felt alone in my search for answers but I was determined to find them.

Meanwhile, in 1976, the year I celebrated my eighteenth birthday, I received a notice to appear before the draft board for a medical exam. I was conflicted about serving in the military because my father's behavior was a daily reminder of the destructive lifelong impact military service can have. Tales of glory and honor were mixed with his somber descriptions of destruction and human suffering whose impact I could feel in the depth of his silences. My mother had forbade me as a child from playing war games, and I will never forget my father's warnings about the danger of guns.

During one of our hunting trips, I carelessly handled an unloaded shotgun, pointing it in the direction of a fellow hunter. My father castigated me, saying that a gun is by definition a dangerous tool and must never be pointed in the direction of another human being. This was one of the few moments when I admired my father, beyond his military accomplishment. In hindsight he at least appeared to make a conscious effort to distant himself and learn from his past actions, or at least to impress upon me the dangers of weapons when they are not handled properly.

Could I follow an order to raise a weapon against a fellow human being? *Should* I follow orders in an army so tainted by its past? I knew that at least several senior commanding officers in the new German army were former Wehrmacht officers, and many military barracks were named after German war "heroes" of the Second World War. I therefore decided to refuse to serve in the armed forces. Such a refusal was permitted by German law, but required a written explanation, a hearing in front of the draft board, and the commitment to perform civil service for a period exceeding the length of mandatory military service by at least three months.

Anticipating a heated conflict with my father over the issue, I kept my intentions well hidden – until the day he found out on his own. I suspect that he either opened my mail or received a call from on of his friends within the military establishment.

He summoned me to the living room and was sitting at the table holding a cigar in his left hand. An empty wine glass was on the table, but because the bottle on the floor behind the chair was not yet empty, I thought that his tone might not be too severe. In the last few years my father's alcoholism had worsened. He would often drink during the day, developing a dull daze by early evening that prevented any chance of a productive conversation. I believe that he was still trying to control his drinking habits of his own volition; later he drifted in an abyss of raw anger and lengthening drunken stupors that would eventually dissolve our relationship.

He looked at me with his dark brown eyes and said, "I have spoken with the chair of the draft board and he told me about your intentions. You understand that I am disappointed."

He paused briefly and then continued.

"Nevertheless, I understand you. You have witnessed the pain and suffering that the war has brought to our own family and ..."

I interrupted him, testing my boundaries.

"You mean, what you have brought to yourself and our family."

"Let me continue," he said. "I understand your motivation and I know that you are an idealistic, responsible and sensitive young man. I see some of myself in you. You may not believe me, but I was like you at one time; we are not so different, you know. Unfortunately, I believed in ideas that were later proven wrong. I believed in my fatherland and in my duty to defend it against all enemies. This belief led me to join the German army at the age of twenty. I fought with honor and as an officer I was bound by an oath of loyalty to Adolf Hitler and to my country. After the war I was imprisoned by the Americans and came to the realization that my service had been in vain and that my honor as an officer had been disgraced by those criminals in Berlin. Those cowards abused Germany, they abused our people, they abused me, and then they took their own lives, leaving us to clean up the mess they left behind. Even though I am still a reserve officer, I understand your decision not to serve. I have decided that I will write a letter to the draft board to support your application for deferment and your willingness to fulfill an alternative civil service obligation."

I stared at him in disbelief. At that moment, for perhaps the first time in my adult life, I felt that I had a father.

"I just don't know what to say...." I said.

But he waved his hands to stop me.

"There is no need to get emotional," he said. "This needs to be handled and you know your responsibilities. You will have to serve your country in another way and I have no doubt that you will do so, but now you better leave me alone." With that he turned his head away.

For a fleeting moment we were close to connecting as father and son, but he seemed to close the door on that opportunity almost as soon as it opened. Neither of us knew that this would be our last opportunity to reconcile, and we failed to seize it. We hung there, suspended in silence, our two minds pushing each other away like two magnetic poles when they got too close.

My father kept his word and wrote a long letter to the draft board expressing his concerns and opinions in a typically controlled and measured manner. I saved a copy of the letter and have read it many times since.

I still remember one of the sentences in his letter until today;

"I was fighting for my beloved fatherland, lost my friends and almost my life, only to be left in disgrace and shame after the war. Those who claimed to lead us cowardly escaped by either committing suicide or leaving Germany for faraway lands. I stayed and realize today that my son has the right to raise those questions I was unable or unwilling to ask."

I wished then, and still do, that he would have had the courage and strength to face Germany's historic responsibility for the horrific crimes committed in its name. It was now left to me to step forward seeking answers.

In May, 1978, I completed gymnasium, a preparatory school to a higher education at university. I graduated with honors, as one of the top three students in the class. My grades allowed me to join any university program I wished. I chose a program within the medical profession because I knew I would gain credentials I could use anywhere, and as an added benefit, the government permitted every student of medicine or dentistry to defer their service commitment until the completion of graduate studies. I gladly accepted that deferment and began my studies.

I was searching for independence and had already thought about leaving Germany one day to explore the world. A medical degree would provide me with the professional independence to earn a living anywhere.

In late summer of that same year, I was accepted by the dental school and started my studies in October 1978 at the University of Bonn.

I was young and naïve. I did not know what I wanted from life and was unaware of my abilities and limitations. I was attracted to politics, philosophy, sociology, and religion, but I also liked also biology and natural sciences. I was torn between following my heart or a more practical course, and did not know how to choose. I decided, by default, to begin the study of dentistry. That decision pleased and surprised my parents, who figured that I would prefer something like sociology. This state of affairs did not last long.

In January 1979 the American TV series "Holocaust" was shown in its entirety, breaking a thirty-five-year taboo in West Germany on programs about the Nazi past and the atrocities committed by Germans in the name of Germany. Millions of Germans tuned in and many learned for the first time about what had actually taken place.

The wall of silence crumbled and for the first time questions began to be asked openly.

My father's reaction was predictable.

"Nobody in this house will watch this program," he yelled.

"This is just another smear campaign by those Jews in Hollywood and we don't have to listen to their lies." My father continued to deny the overwhelming facts about the systematic mass murder of Jews and called the Holocaust a "lie."

He prevented me from watching the TV program at home, so I had to read about it in newspapers and magazines. I was deeply shocked to read how the systematic elimination and murder of an entire people had been ordered and implemented by Germans.

I learned for the first time such names as Eichmann and Mengele, and the truth that Jews were not merely victims of the war, like everyone else, but targets for death for no other reason their being Jewish.

Despite my fear of his anger, I couldn't resist asking my father about his knowledge of the events and his role in the war. I entered his study in our new spacious house in Meckenheim and found him sitting at his elegant, polished oak table. He looked at me over the rims of his glasses with sad eyes.

"I know why you are here," he said.

"If you know, why don't you tell me your version of what has happened. I would like to at least hear it from you personally," I replied.

He hesitated, then spoke without looking me in the eye

"I was a young man," he said, "a proud officer fighting for my country. I felt I was doing the right thing by serving in the army as my father and grandfather had done before me. I never imagined that these things could happen."

He reclined in his chair, his head turning to the side and his hand holding a glass of wine, which probably helped him loosen up. I was certain it was not his first glass that day.

"We entered Poland and then Russia. We were the front-line troops and fought against armies, not civilians. We never intentionally killed or targeted civilians. The SS troops came in after us to clean up the mess. I never knew what their actions were nor what their presence meant, nor did I ask. They were not real soldiers like us. They had not the same military training like us and I never liked them. They did there job and we did ours. One day when I was returning to Germany from the front in Russia, our train stopped in a station in Poland. On the other side of the station I saw some cattle cars filled with civilians, mostly women and children. They were silent; no one was screaming. We were heading West and they were heading East. One of my friends said that those civilians were Jews being resettled in the East, but we all knew there were no preparations to resettle them. We knew that the SS troops were cleaning up villages by rounding up civilians, killing them, and burning their bodies. I saw the smoke clouds and smelled burning flesh. Rumors were circulating among the troops about concentration camps in the East, but we knew no details. To us they were just rumors."

His voice was trembling; he almost sounded as though he was pleading with me.

"I know you want to know more. Believe me when I say I did not know much of this until after the war."

This was hard to believe, and I suspected that even in retrospect my father was camouflaging what he knew.

"I tried to forget so many things and to shelter my family from all of that. We need to forget and move on and not reopen all of these old wounds. Doing so will help no one!"

At that point I stopped him.

"I think you were wrong for not telling me all these years. I had to find out for myself, and I think you were wrong not to tell me. We cannot just forget and move on as if all of this never happened. It did happen, and those who suffered deserve to have their story told. You have taught me to bear responsibility as an individual. Now it's time to bear collective responsibility and face the consequences of those actions."

His body stiffened as if to respond harshly, but the alcohol blunted his edge.

"What are you taking about? Nobody will be helped with that. You are my son and I know that I have failed to make you understand my way of thinking. You have your own mind and you are as hardheaded as I am. I believe that I did nothing wrong. In fact, I helped your uncle to get out of a concentration camp."

I was stunned and surprised. I knew nothing about this. My mother had told me about this uncle, but we had never met. My father continued,

"Yes, my brother Karl. He was the black sheep of the family. As a communist sympathizer he was imprisoned in a concentration camp in Bavaria. He deserved it, because he couldn't keep his big mouth shut. Your mother and my sister Ursel urged me to help him so I traveled to Dachau. As a decorated army officer wearing the Knight's cross, I was able to persuade the camp commander to release my brother. I risked my entire career for this idiot, but I knew that otherwise he would have been killed. As it was, he was almost starved when I got there. I'll never forget that moment. He was a walking skeleton and I did not even recognize him at first. I made him promise in front of the camp commander, a man I knew personally from NAPOLA school, to never come in contact with any Communist ever again. I took personal responsibility for his future behavior. Yes, I knew about the camps. But no, I did not know how they killed people nor I do not want to know now. The war is over."

My father looked exhausted as he sank deeper into his chair. I was amazed and even grateful to hear this story, and for the first time in my life I felt genuine pity for him.

"Father," I said, "please understand that I need to know more about this. I intend to travel to Israel to learn more about the history... our history."

At first he did not react, but slowly lifted his head.

"I cannot stop you from doing what you will, but be careful what side you pick – your own family or those Jews. The choice is yours."

I was taken aback by his unveiled threat but I felt my own strength and spoke freely.

"I only know that I have decided to find the truth."

It was at this point that I noticed the alcohol had taken over and that I had best to leave the room.

CHAPTER 2

THE ROAD TO JERUSALEM

A S I WAS MOVING full-time into spending all of my time pursuing the study of dentistry, I was having second thoughts about continuing in that direction. Did I choose this profession just to be independent, or was it a career where I could find lifetime fulfillment? I was a lousy technician and always seemed to be performing below the level of my classmates. I was frustrated and looking forward to the semester break. I had more never lost interest in reading for pleasure and spent all my spare time devouring books and other readings materials as much as time would permit. I had subscribed to a progressive interfaith magazine and I found a short article announcing a peace conference in the nearby city of Koblenz, comprised of Jewish and Arab youth from Israel.

The mission was organized by Neve Shalom, a movement based in the Jewish/Arab village of that name Neve Shalom, which was also known as the "Oasis of Peace,", or Wahat as-Salam in Arabic. The article mentioned that the village was founded by Bruno Hussar, an Egyptian-born Jew who converted to Catholicism and became a Dominican monk. Father Hussar had come to Israel in 1960 to establish a Catholic center for the study of Judaism. It was his belief that a substantial part of the Arab-Israeli problem had grown out of, or was due to, a basic cultural and religious misunderstanding. He sought to build a Christian-Jewish-Muslim spiritual community that would model peaceful coexistence. He founded Neve Shalom in 1972 on 120 acres of land leased from the nearby Latrun Monastery, half-way between Tel Aviv and Jerusalem, where many Jewish refugees from Eastern Europe spending their first and for some the last weeks of their lives in this land fighting and dying on that hillside to reestablish the State of Israel. In its first years, Hussar lived alone on the hilltop in a bus with no running water or electricity. He had many Israeli and Palestinian visitors, but few of them wanted to settle on the hillside. Interest in his project grew over time, however, and in 1977, he gave the first course in conflict resolution for Jewish and Arab high school students. The first five families settled there in 1978, four Jewish and one Palestinian. Their objective was building a network of Jews and Arabs committed to co-existing in a shared community. I was immediately drawn to the idea, because I had known about and studied the same Israeli-Palestinian conflict, that was brought to my country by way of the Olympic killings of 1972.

I knew that I wanted to be at that conference, which had already begun the day before I read the announcement. I had to decide quickly what to do. Little did I know how radically that decision would shape my life.

The conference was held just a few miles outside Koblenz, a city on the left bank of the Rhine river at its confluence with the Moselle. I had very little money, so I decided to hitchhike from my house to Koblenz and to take a bus or train from there.

My journey began on the ramp of the autobahn heading south to Koblenz where I was lucky enough to catch a ride that took me directly to Koblenz. A connecting bus dropped me off near the conference center.

Soon I was walking up the road leading to a small hotel huddled on the slope of a vineyard. The gate to the parking lot was open and I heard a choir of voices singing loudly in the same strange language I had heard during the funeral of the murdered Israeli athletes. By then I knew it was Ivrith, or modern Hebrew. When I reached the front yard of the hotel, a group of young men and women were dancing and singing and smiling broadly. Their shared expressions reminded me of smiles I had seen on the faces of the Israelis marching into the Olympic stadium in Munich.

That was when I first saw her. A tall, blond, stunningly beautiful girl who seemed to lead the group of dancing and singing Israelis. I was powerfully drawn to her. As I approached, a muscular, dark-haired young man stopped me and asked me suspiciously who I was and what I was doing there. I smiled and replied,

"Shalom. I am here to participate in the peace mission." I told him that I was a German and had learned about the conference from a journal. He shook my hand and introduced himself.

"My name is Roni and you have to speak with Elias over there."

He pointed to a short, thin man of dark complexion and grayish curly hair. I approached him, introduced myself, and told him of my interest in joining the group.

Elias Jabbour was the charismatic leader of this group of almost two dozen young Arab and Jewish youths from Israel. He was the director of the House of Hope, International Peace Center, in Shefar'Am, an Israeli-Arab village in northern Israel.

The House of Hope was founded in 1978 as a non-profit organization dedicated to the advancement of peace and cooperation based on mutual understanding between Arabs and Jews. Elias saw my genuine enthusiasm to join the group and invited me to follow him into the hotel.

He led me to a small conference room filled with people who were chatting and laughing They ignored me completely. Elias clapped his hands and drew all eyes toward me as I stood next to him.

"Listen, everybody. I have a guest here from Germany who would like to join our group." He asked me to introduce myself. I hesitated, then said,

"Hello, my name is Bernd. I was born in Germany and live not far from here in Bonn. I am here to learn about you and your country."

Everyone applauded politely and immediately returned to their conversations.

Elias turned to a man named Martin who was approaching him with a question. I began to feel out of place, but then someone tapped me on the shoulder and I turned to find it was her, the beautiful blond woman I had admired a few minutes earlier. I can still remember her smile as she looked at me through blue eyes. In English with a Hebrew accent, she said,

"My name is Vered. I am happy to meet you. My mother was born in Romania, and learned to speak German, but I am sorry to say that she never taught me. Let me introduce you to the others."

"What does Vered mean?" I asked.

"Oh, it means Rose, like the flower." she laughed. She took my hand and continued to hold it until I had met every member of the group. Almost all of them, including Vered, had recently finished high school and were about to enter the army. Most of the Jewish members came from Lod, Tel Aviv, and Haifa, and the others were Muslims and Christian Palestinian Arabs from Shfar Am and Abu Gosh, a large Palestinian village nearby Jerusalem. Vered didn't leave my side, and I had no intention of leaving hers.

For the remainder of the afternoon we attended workshops together to discuss the peace process, Israeli and Arab coexistence, and the prospects for a better future.

Everybody was optimistic about achieving peace, which surprised me, but I quickly came to understand that the Israeli-Egypt Peace Treaty of March 1979 had brought new hope to the region, and that hopeful feeling was the foundation of the entire meeting.

Vered and I were assigned to a workshop with three other participants, all of them Israeli-Arabs. One was Chalid, a young-looking, energetic, and intelligent Palestinian student from Abu Gosh, with whom I later developed a deep and lasting friendship. He was quite articulate and drew me into heated discussions. He attended an Israeli high school along with Jewish students and was fluent in Hebrew and English.

I also noticed quickly that he was filled with anger and resentment at being treated as a second-class citizen in Israel.

"I have no future in Israel," he told me. "As an Arab, it's going to be almost impossible for me to attend an Israeli university. Jews are always chosen ahead of any Palestinian and they are always suspicious of us."

"Why are you so angry?" Vered interrupted. "You have been given every opportunity to succeed in Israel, just like I did. It's up to you to make something out of it. Why do you people constantly live in the past? We have a bright future! Even President Sadat came from Egypt to Israel to bring peace. What more do you want?"

This didn't sit well with Chalid and his immediate response was one of anger and frustration.

"Sadat is a traitor! He sold out Palestine. Egypt and Israel made peace but we Palestinians were left out of the equation."

He was referring to the Camp David Accord of September 1978, which defined a new relationship between Egypt and Israel, but failed to do the same for the Palestinians. Actually, both parties agreed on a format to negotiate an autonomous regime in the West Bank and Gaza, but set no date for the negotiations.

This was the first time I experienced the width of the gap between Jews and Arabs in Israel. Both were citizens of the same state, yet each had a very different view of what was taking place. I was learning that there were two peoples who lived in the same place yet had very different experiences of life.

After Chalid's heated reply, Vered appeared angry and upset. When I asked her why, she said

"I'm frustrated and disappointed. I thought we might finally live in peace."

"Have you ever been to an Arab village?" I asked. She looked at me wide-eyed.

"That's too dangerous! Do you have any idea how they treat women in their society? I could never feel safe there."

So she had made it even clearer: two people living in one state, side by side, but separated by a cultural divide that was as wide and as broad as any ocean. How could they ever understand one another if they only had their own experiences as a basis for judgment?

Night was approaching and Vered and I said goodnight. I was assigned to a dormitory room with Chalid and Nabil, another Israeli Arab from Shfar Am. I was too excited to fall asleep and lay awake staring into the darkness.

"I can't sleep either," Chalid said suddenly. "Tell me what you are doing here. You are not Jewish, are you?"

"No, I am not," I replied. "I am here because I'm curious and want to learn more about Israel and the Middle East, Arabs and Jews. I want to learn everything about all of that."

"Why do you?" he said. "Israel is such a mess. Have you ever been there?"

"No, I haven't … not yet. Maybe I will. I think I would like too."

"Come visit my village and I will show you around. I mean it. We Arabs always open our homes to other people."

"Maybe I will," I replied, not knowing yet that Arab hospitality is not just a word but a basic part of their culture.

"I guess you have the hots for the Jewish girl, huh? I saw you looking at her.

Be careful. They are all honey pots you know." Chalid was teasing me and I was glad that he didn't see me blushing. He was right, I was infatuated with her, but I would not admit that to him.

"No, we are just becoming friends. She seems very nice."

"Well, I hope so. I heard that she has a boyfriend. The big guy, I think Roni is his name. Don't mess with him. I would not want to be on his bad side if I were you, Bernd. And besides, Israeli girls always seem easy and friendly, but don't confuse their friendly behavior with any serious intentions. They just like play with guys like you."

"How do you know? I thought you didn't hang out with Jews.'

He turned toward me and I felt his eyes staring at me in the darkness.

"Let's make one thing clear, please. I have nothing against Jews. I grew up with them, went to school with them, work with them and live with them. But we are two different people living in one state. I will never date a Jewish girl because they neither respect nor understand my culture, and I don't want my kids to be Jewish. Its as simple as that."

"Now that sounded really racist. Imagine if I as a German had said that.

Everybody would call me a Nazi or at the very least a racist, I replied.

"Well, my friend. You Germans have a problem with the Jews, because you killed them. Now you feel guilty about it and expect others to feel the same guilt and pity for Jews that you feel. We Palestinians suffered all our lives from what the Jews did to us. You cannot expect me to like them and you can not expect me to share your guilt."

Our conversation woke Nabil and he growled at us to shut up and go to sleep.

He was right. We would have many more opportunities to discuss all of this and much more before our time was done.

"Good night," I said. "*Laila tiaba,* good night, "Chalid replied.

It was Saturday morning and the sun lit the Rhine Valley with bright but soft morning light. The dew was dripping off the leaves and the early morning fog was slowly melting to reveal a stunning view of the river Rhine River below. Large barges pushed their heavy loads upstream and small tour boats carried eager passengers upriver to catch a glimpse of the castles on the slopes of the hills framing the river.

The Rhine valley has always been an important artery of communication, commerce, and transportation in Germany. Roman and German emperors recognized its vital strategic importance, and in the middle ages warlords built castles to control the flow of goods and maintain visual command and vantage points, and also to regulate the flow of traffic and levy tolls on merchants. This accounts for the large number of castles along the Rhein from Mainz to Bonn, particularly in the narrow gorge connecting Bingen and Koblenz. Along this stretch of river, our group was going to tour the town of Bingen, founded by Romans nearly 2000 years ago. Jews settled in the town in the 12th century AD and the Jewish community grew to almost 800 during the early 1900s. Many Jewish citizens left after the rise of the Nazi dictatorship, and most of those who did not were deported to concentration camps and murdered. All that remained were Jewish cemeteries, a sad reality repeated throughout Germany. Many of those cemeteries are maintained by Germans dedicated to keeping alive the memory of Jewish life in their city.

It was late morning when we arrived. The city's medieval architecture was picturesque, and our first stop was at a small church. Vered was hanging out with her friends and I had to admit that I felt somewhat ignored by her. I stayed close to Chalid and Nabil and tried to seem occupied and content. Both of them were Muslims and neither had ever set foot in a church.

"You must feel at home in this house of God," Chalid remarked to me.

"To tell you the truth," I replied, "I haven't been in a church for over twelve years; since my holy communion."

"Why not?" he asked.

"Well, I never found any real spiritual connection in the church. I just went because I was supposed to go."

"What are you looking for?" he persisted.

"Complete inner peace and a sense of feeling at home might be nice for starters. I don't belong to the Catholic church, even though I was born Catholic."

"Are you attracted towards Judaism? Do you want to become a Jew? It seems to me that you are."

His question startled me because he had so quickly grasped the complex search for my own reality. Is this what I had been thinking and had only begun to realize? Did I really want to take this step or did I merely like the thought of it? In the end, some changes are best left imagined and unfulfilled. How could I be certain I was doing the right thing and being true to myself, my family, and my future? Was I seeking to change religion, in order to remove feelings of guilt by association, or were my motivations more genuine than that? I knew that Judaism was more than a religion. It was a culture and a people.

It would mean making a complete break with my family, from life as I had known it, and probably from Germany as well.

I was not sure how to answer his question, but something more important happened: His question became my question, and I felt myself taking on that entire dilemma. I simply said,

"I don't know what to say. I haven't thought it through."

He made a face and rolled his eyes. "Not only did I make another Jew; I did it in a church. May Allah forgive me."

In the evening we returned to the hotel and met for dinner.

I searched for Vered and sat next to her. She looked at me with those beautiful bright blue eyes and asked what I had been doing.

"Well, I really enjoyed myself today, but I am afraid that I have to leave tomorrow. I have to return to my studies at the University."

"Why so soon? Don't you like it here? Don't you want to spend more time with us? With me?"

She looked down at her plate and for the first time appeared sad.

"You know, this trip is very important for me and I am glad I met you, " she said.

"I grew up knowing about the horrors that were inflicted on my people here in Germany and I was always curious about how Germans today actually feel about it. I told you that my mother is from Romania, but I never knew my father. He disappeared when I was born, leaving my mother alone. I grew up in very simple circumstances and we still live in a small apartment. My mom met another man and he is like a father to me. Nazis killed most of my mother's family and you are the first German I have ever met. The fact that I even like you is amazing to me."

She looked up, faced me and for the first time I saw tears in her eyes.

"Please, let's stay in touch, okay? I would like you to visit me and my family in Israel. There is so much we can talk about. Will you come?'

"Yes, I will come," I promised without even knowing how or when I could arrange such a trip. Israel seemed so far away, but looking in her eyes I knew it was not too far.

"When are you going to leave us?" she asked.

"Tomorrow, early in the morning."

"Will you have time to say good-bye?"

"I think it's better to do that now."

Her faced moved close to mine and our lips almost touched.

"I'll see you in Israel. You promise?"

"I promise."

She kissed me on my cheek, stood up, and left the table.

Chalid, who had watched us from the other table, came over and sat down.

"You are in big trouble, my friend. I see you got bitten by the love bug."

"Maybe, but at least now I have a reason for traveling to Israel."

"You had a reason before. You are very curious, and something powerful drives you in your search to know more about the Jews. I hope it's not guilt, because there are many things in Israel that can make a man feel guilty." I heard the bitterness in his last remark.

"Don't forget Bernd, you are a German, and they will always blame you for what happened to them. But of course nobody will mention what happened to us Palestinians as a result of the Jewish occupation of Palestine. We are left to suffer under Israeli rule – because of what you Germans did to the Jews. That is how it is."

His words got to me.

"I thought you came here to learn about peaceful coexistence. Why do you speak with such tones of resentment and revenge?"

"You're so naive, Bernd. You haven't seen anything yet. Don't forget that the Palestinians don't live together with Jews by choice. We're forced to! I would like you to visit my village to learn both sides of the story. Don't let yourself be led to false conclusions by beautiful Israeli girls."

He was visibly angry, but I suspected that a trip to Israel would be a challenging and worthwhile learning experience for both of us.

After my return home, Israel and Vered remained in my thoughts as I started planning my trip to Israel. But I still faced my training and study, which I didn't enjoy. I had no money for any such trip and I became increasingly frustrated and angry at my circumstances.

I needed to ask for help and there was no one other than my father to turn to. Of course I found the idea of asking him for help very distasteful. I avoided the conversation for some time because it would force my negative feelings towards him to surface. To me, our difficulties were at least partly due to his authoritarian education.

At the same time, my own sensitivity to our failing relationship was a real part of who I was and why we were indeed at odds with each other. I realized that he had little tolerance for my sentiments, which he considered a clear sign of weakness.

He must have had feelings he could have communicated, but he would not reveal them to me. My mother seemed able to live with this lack of emotional warmth and attention and to a great extent she compensated by focusing on me. This led to an overprotective environment as she often tried to shelter me from outside harm and bad influences, much to my irritation.

My inability to communicate with my father lead to a tense and muted atmosphere in our home. I often retreated to my room for hours at a time – partly to read and study, but mostly to avoid exasperating conversations with my parents. When speaking with my father, I avoided going beyond simple small talk.

I became tense and unable to find the right words. I inevitably began babbling about my studies, pretending that I enjoyed them. This was intended to please him and soften him up for the topics I really wanted to discuss. In particular, I needed him to be in the right frame of mind to broach a financial discussion. That would require catching him in that narrow window each day between light alcoholic euphoria and drunken stupor. Once the window closed, it was too late to have a conversation.

Prior to his retirement from the German Ministry he always told us how much he would enjoy having time to focus on gardening, hunting, walking and reading. But in reality he just slipped deeper and deeper into those big bottles of cheap Italian wine he drank every day. Before his retirement I hardly ever saw him drink before early evening, but now he started in the early afternoon and was often quiet and sullen by dinnertime. This of course created greater distance between us and further reduced our chances of having a meaningful conversation.

I remember watching him one day from the window of my bedroom. He was walking in a small garden he had planted, carefully observing the weary products of his neglected horticultural experiments. His gardening skills were marginal and his plants were stunted, undernourished, and weak. Nevertheless, we had to praise him for his efforts or he would use the perceived criticism as reason to pour another drink.

From the window I could see that he was smoking one of the cheap cigars he liked. I could almost smell the disagreeable odor from my room. But at least he appeared sober, and I knew that the late afternoon hour presented the best opportunity to speak with him about my agenda. I flew down the stairs and checked the fridge. A huge bottle of wine was still chilling, waiting to be emptied. This suggested that he had not yet begun. I left the house and entered the garden, trying to seem relaxed and happy to meet him. I must have appeared tense, however, because he looked at me disapprovingly. He seemed able to read me so easily.

"You want something," he announced. "What is it?" His disapproving stare and my searching eyes met for a moment and seemed to almost bounce off each other, leaving our eyes as unconnected as our personalities.

I gathered my strength and forced a phony smile.

"I need money for my studies," I lied.

He saw through it immediately.

"Where do you want to study? Israel? Look Bernd, I know that this is about Israel and I am trying to figure out how you got so obsessed with this ridiculous idea. Can you possibly explain that to me please?"

Having failed to hide the truth, I felt embarrassed and exposed.

"I need to know the truth," I answered, "but nobody is telling me, so I need to find it myself."

"What truth?" he asked. "I've told you many times. We had nothing to do with what happened to the Jews. And what is done is done. Let the past rest. We need to move on. We all need to move on. I admit that I admire the Israelis. They are different than the Jews we knew here in Germany. They are tough. They fight and work hard for their own survival and I respect them for that. But please let me alone with all of this talk and ridiculous sentiment about the Jews. They are gone from here and they should be forgotten."

This was unusual; I seldom heard so many words from him. But he seemed to welcome the opportunity. Perhaps, he realized, he too needed to talk about this issue.

"Sometime around 1965, I met some Israeli officers who were studying our Blitzkrieg tactics," he continued.

"They were young and very bright individuals. Real quick learners. We taught them everything they needed to know. They even studied the original Clausewitz strategies of war. I firmly believe that they applied that knowledge in the Six-Day War in 1967 and it was a relevant factor in their success. A real Blitzkrieg success, you might say. I had a difficult time believing that the Jews fought that well. Then they did it again in 1973."

I kept silent and hoped for more. I knew that Israel's military capability appealed to his deep-rooted sense of military tradition. He could identify with the fighting Jew, but still held on to the stereotype of the Jew he had learned about long ago in the NAPOLA.

Finally I spoke.

"Father, help me get to know them and understand who they are. Help me travel to Israel." My words seemed to move him in a way I seldom saw, though I could not tell in what direction. After a few tense moments of silence he replied,

"I know I cannot stop you. You will do what you want to do regardless of what I say, feel, or think. Go and form your opinion on your own. I lost my son a long time ago."

He paused.

"I will make certain your mother has the money. I do not wish to give it to you directly. I would rather that she did." With those words hanging uncertainly in the air between us, he turned and walked back to the house.

I was simultaneously relieved, saddened, and shocked. I felt like the breath had been knocked out of me. I had achieved my goal, but at what cost? My father had told me that I was lost to him; did it not follow that he, too, was lost to me? What had I done to earn this judgment from my own father? Even though the distance between us continued to grow, I still respected him as my father and at many levels felt everything a son feels for his dad. Why was he rejecting me? Yes, I wanted answers, and I did not want to wait, but why should that cost me his love?

In the coming days the tension continued to grow. Soon he stopped talking to me altogether. Through all of this my mother suffered greatly. One day she approached me with tears in her eyes, clutching an envelope.

"Your father gave me some money for you. I know you will need more than that so I added some from my savings."

I was well aware that my father was keeping her on a very short financial leash because he liked to control her. She must have saved this money over the course of several years and now she was giving it to me to enable my travel to Israel.

I'm not certain whether her next words were what she believed or were just her way of standing behind a son when he needed her most.

"You need to find the answers to your questions," she said. "I know there is a connection between you and them. I can only guess why. My parents told me little about any of this, and I too was left wondering. I am a good Catholic and I truly believed that by baptizing you I could show you a different direction and a different life. But deep in your heart you have discovered a spark that lit this fire of curiosity. I guess I always knew it might happen some time with someone in our family. I was afraid that it would be you."

"Mother," I pleaded, "What are you saying? Please tell me truth! Tell me who you are and why you are telling me this."

Tears came to her eyes and she hugged me tight. She pressed her lips close to my ears and whispered,

" Forgive me, because I have sinned. Write a prayer on a piece of paper and place it between the stones of the Wall in Jerusalem. Don't forget! Do that for me please."

She appeared exhausted and drained, and I felt her slip away from me. She glanced nervously glancing around, afraid that my father might have overheard our conversation.

I was confused and overwhelmed by all this, and did not know what else to say to her. I held the envelope in my hand, guessing that the answer to my questions might not be as far away as I had thought. But already my mother had sunk back into silence and left me guessing about the meaning of what had just taken place. What was my mother trying to say? Who am I? Why had that subject opened and just as suddenly closed? I knew that my mother was a devout Catholic, but was there any truth to the rumors that my maternal ancestors might have been Jewish?

I never found the answer to this important question, but searching for it revealed a new and exciting world of prayer and thoughts. It also confirmed my need to travel to Israel to learn as much as I could about myself.

THE JOURNEY BEGINS

MY DECISION TO LEAVE for Israel energized me and I moved quickly to push my dream toward reality. In 1978, traveling by plane was beyond my limited budget, so my journey would be by boat and train. The best route, I decided, began with a long train ride from Bonn to the Italian seaport of Ancona, situated on the Adriatic Sea in the northeastern part of Italy. From there I would board a ferry to Greece and then finally on to Israel. The entire trip from Germany to Israel would take four days and five nights. My stay in Israel would be only five or six days, but I did not mind. It was infinitely better than no trip at all, and I prepared as thoroughly as could. I was eager to share my excitement with my father, but as my departure approached he withdrew even deeper within himself and seemed to drink even more.

My mother was aware of my eagerness to talk about my hopes and dreams for this trip, but she also sensed that it might change my life, and in that she was right. The journey would change me forever. As my departure date approached, the journey was taking on a life and inevitability of its own. This was a realization that was at once alarming and exhilarating.

One evening the phone rang and my father answered it. He shouted up to me immediately:

"Come down here, Bernd, and hurry. You have a call from Israel." I flew down the stairs and grabbed the receiver from his hand. His face showed no expression as he immediately turned away from me.

"Hello, who is this?" I asked, then recognized her voice immediately.

"It's me, Vered. How are you doing? I missed you and wanted to hear your voice."

"I'm fine. It's nice to hear from you. In fact, I am getting ready to leave."

"Where are you going?"

"I just bought the tickets and am leaving for Israel on Sunday."

After a short moment of silence she started to cheer and cry at once.

"I cannot believe it! You are really coming? You must stay in my parent's house. I want to show you my country. When are you arriving?"

"I'm taking the train and a ferry and should be there on Thursday of next week. Probably around noontime, depending on the weather," I replied.

"Don't worry. I will check the arrival times. Oh my God, I cannot believe it. You are coming. I *will* see you again!"

As she hung up, I stood motionless for a moment holding the receiver in my hand. I did not notice that my father was still in the room and had obviously listened to the conversation.

"So, it's a woman that drives you to Israel," he said sourly. "I knew it was something other than their religion."

"You are wrong father. It's more than a woman. Something in my heart tells me that I belong there."

His face turned red and his voice rumbled into its threatening mode.

"I did not raise you to be a Jew-lover. You will see that they cannot manage their own lives and are always getting themselves into trouble for that very reason."

I couldn't control my response.

"In trouble? You mean getting killed for being Jews? Is that the trouble you are referring to?"

He was in an alcohol-powered rage now. His voice trembled and his hands shook. "You will never set a foot in this house again if you get involved with a Jew girl."

I managed to hold my temper and remained silent, then turned to climb the stairs to my room.

He was yelling again.

"Answer me, God damn you. Answer me now!" I turned and stared into his dark, bloodshot eyes. I wished I could talk to him reasonably and express my feelings in a way he could at least understand, even if he could not agree. But I knew that he would not understand, and of course he would never agree.

"I will not talk to you now. Not under these circumstances. Go back to the other room and crawl into your bottle."

He listened to what I said and I was surprised by his restrained reaction as his eyes glimmered with sorrow for a few seconds. But the glow quickly faded, replaced by that hated dark and detached expression.

"So be it," he said, turning on his heels and slamming the door behind him

DEPARTURE

THE BACKPACK WAS READY, leaning against my chair, the sleeping bag tied securely. I knew I wouldn't sleep in a bed for quite a while. My passport and money were wrapped tightly together with rubber bands and stuffed into my waist stash. I had never before traveled such a distance, certainly not by long train and boat journeys to an unknown land. I was both excited and fearful. I knew that there was no turning back.

I slept very little the night before the trip and rose early in the morning feeling awake and alive. It was unusual to see my father walking in the garden at that early hour and I wanted to join him, but hesitated. He was puffing nervously on a cigar and pacing up and down the pathway in his small garden. Eventually I found the courage and called to him from the sliding door of the porch, wondering how best to say goodbye.

"Good morning, father. Will you take me to the train station?" He turned around, staring at me with his sad, dark eyes.

"Of course I will son." I was surprised by his agreeable tone. Then I turned toward my mother, who was sitting at the breakfast table, hunched over her cup of coffee, her hair disheveled from a restless night's sleep. She had dark circles under her eyes and was obviously agitated. I felt guilty about leaving her in this state, and only added to that guilt by saying,

"Don't worry Mother. I'll be back."

When she looked at me, I saw that she had been crying. She tried to control her voice, but her words were broken by soft sobs.

"You will see another world, Bernd. One I never saw. You will feel another world that I never felt, and you will experience what it means to go home. Don't forget me. Don't forget us."

I wanted to reassure her that it would all be okay, but she was so upset that I could only think to say that I would not forget her. As I turned to leave she just sat there crying. Without turning back I hurried out the door. My father pulled the car to the front of the house and I slid into the front seat.

We drove toward Bonn without exchanging a word until my father finally broke the silence.

"You are beginning a very challenging journey today. I don't know what you will find, but whatever it is, take care of yourself. You are a very curious and stubborn young man and I cannot stop you from searching for what it is that drives you. Don't forget us. We will be always your parents."

He stopped the car in front of the train station and turned toward me.

"I will drop you here. Stay safe and call if you need me." His voice was soft and his eyes radiated warmth for the first time in many years. For a second I thought I saw tears in his eyes and I wanted to embrace him, to feel physically connected, but he turned his head and waved me away, as he had so many times.

"Father, I will come back soon. Thank you for your help." He said no more as I stepped out of the car, pulled my backpack from the trunk, and began my journey.

As the train left the station, I tried to catch a glimpse of my father's car but he had already left. I sank into my seat and, for the moment, was too excited to reflect on my parent's behavior and their odd words regarding my departure. It was time to go, a time to let go of the restraints that had held me back. I was finally doing what I wanted to do.

After reaching Munich I changed trains for Bologna, Italy, and from there took another train to the port city of Ancona. When I arrived it was mid-morning and the train station was overflowing with people, all in a hurry, chatting and laughing. Children ran between the flood of passengers and one boy almost knocked me over.

"*Scusi signore* – excuse me sir," he grinned and ran off.

I knew that the ferry would leave at 3:00 p.m. It was already 2:00 p.m. and I had no clue how to get to the harbor. I tried asking several people in both English and German, but nobody seemed to understand me. Frustrated and tired, I decided to follow my instincts. I walked down a hill and after a few minutes I smelled the sea and saw seagulls overhead. Suddenly there was the blue Mediterranean and the large ferry itself resting at the pier, ready to take me on my very long journey. I started to run, afraid I would miss the boat, but I made it on time and walked aboard, exhausted but elated.

This huge ship was designed to carry trucks and cars from Italy to Greece and Israel, and the passengers either found seats on a covered area of the top deck or, if that area was full, wherever possible on deck. I was too late to find a seat but did not mind staying on deck. I was more concerned with leaving, and soon the ferry slowly eased away from the dock. The diesel engines sputtered and sprang to life and the huge propellers began pushing the ship toward Israel. I was really on my way, the beginning of my journey.

Settling in on the ship was not difficult, though the amenities on board were few and the food was expensive and tasteless. I still had a sandwich my mother had prepared, and had only to find some fresh water. I started to drink the water from the faucet in the bathroom when a man approached me.

"Don't drink that water. It will make you sick." He was a tall and muscular man in his fifties, with a bushy moustache and curly dark hair. His dark, wrinkled skin made him appear older, but his brown eyes were sparkling and full of life. He eyed me suspiciously, perhaps wondering why anyone would not know better than to drink that water.

"Where are you from and where are you going?" he asked. I stretched out my hand to greet him saying,

"My name is Bernd. I am from Germany and I'm going to Israel."

His expression changed immediately and he neglected to shake my hand.

"Just don't drink that water," he said, turning to leave.

I was surprised at his change in attitude, but now I was beginning to understand what I was up against. I had tried to understand the history and the horrible crimes committed against the Jewish people, but until now I had never felt those conflicts as a part of my own identity. Of course I was German, but I thought that my willingness to learn and experience Israel first-hand would be enough to overcome animosity and resentment. This expectation was of course naïve, and I had to learn to be prepared to listen and understand the reactions of those I was about to meet.

I found a space on deck to lay out my sleeping bag and crawled in for the night. I spent the following day resting in the shadow of the ship's giant stack until hunger and thirst drove me to seek food. I was crossing the deck on my way to the cafeteria when I came across a group of five men. I recognized one of them as the man who advised me not to drink tap water. They were arguing loudly in a language I had learned to identify as Hebrew. As I approached, I noticed they were playing a board game. When I went closer, their conversation stopped. I suddenly found myself the focus of their attention, so I turned to the man I had met the day before.

"I wanted to thank you for the advice you gave me yesterday," I said.

"I have never been on such a ship and wasn't aware that the water was not okay to drink. I am looking for a place to buy water and something to eat right now." He looked at me and must have noticed that I was hungry, thirsty, and tired.

"You are the German guy going to Israel. Here, have a drink," he said handing me a bottle of water.

"Thank you, but I do not want to impose," I replied. He grinned and just pushed the bottle of water into my hands.

"Listen to me, it's a long way to Israel and you are not well prepared. Do yourself a favor and take this bottle. During our stop in Piraeus, fill it with water and buy some extra bottles, bread, olives and cheese for the remainder of the trip to Haifa. The food on this ship is bad and too expensive."

I was grateful for his advice and kindness. I extended my hand and asked his name. This time he shook my hand and said in German.

"My name is Moshe and you are Bernd. Is that right?" Surprised by his flawless German accent I asked,

"How did you learn to speak German?" He looked straight at me and said,

"I was born in Frankfurt. My life there ended with Kristallnacht, euphemistically called the night of the broken glasses, when Nazi gangs smashed my father's business. Soon afterwards he sent me to England to stay with a friend of the family. I never saw my own family again. All of them, my parents, sisters and brothers, were murdered in Auschwitz."

As he told me his life story, he continued to hold my hand, and with every word his grip grew tighter. I am certain he noticed my painful expression, and perhaps knew that it was only partly caused by his grip. Most of what I felt came from his story, which brought home all I had read, all I had feared, in a more powerful way. I had read about the horrors of Auschwitz, the selections, gas chambers, ovens, and the millions of people who were murdered there. So many millions that the individual victims were faceless. Now I was face to face with somebody who had been directly affected by the horrors.

Although he would certainly not be the last, I would never forget this meeting.

"I never thought I would speak to a German again," he was saying, "but you seem to be okay. Come on, I'll introduce you to the others." The four men had left, so I followed Moshe to the dinning room. He stopped at a table where the other men were having a meal. One of them spoke with Moshe in Hebrew, and his tone of voice and gestures made it clear that the conversation was about me. Moshe remained quiet and then turned to me.

"Let me introduce you. Just relax, okay? Meet Chaim, Rafi, Uri, and Doron. My friends, this is Bernd. He is from Germany and he seems to be hungry." None of the men seemed overjoyed to meet me, but grudgingly the man closest to me moved just enough to allow me to sit with them. All of them seemed to notice that I was nervous, and again Moshe broke the silence.

"Let's get him something to eat. This boy looks hungry."

The man named Doron sat upright, his muscular arms crossed over his chest. On his right arm were visible a tattoo with a letter and number. I could not help but stare at the tattoo. He leaned forward, his eyes piercing me, and pressed each word between his clutched teeth as he talked.

"That's a present I received from Germany. I was just fifteen when your people destroyed my life. My entire family was deported to Auschwitz and I was the only one to survive." He lifted his right arm and held it before my eyes.

"That number reminds me every day of my past. You have no idea what that means, do you?" He sank back into his seat and fell silent. A tense silence settled over the table, and I felt uncomfortable, angry, and sad – angry about my father and about the people who did what they did. I couldn't change the past, so I was forced to live with it and to pay this price for being a German. My father was a permanent reminder of how the war had complicated my life, but I could not begin to compare my situation with those of the victims around me. My heart was pounding and I could not look the men in the eyes any more.

I was about to stand and leave when Moshe put his hands on

my shoulders and pushed me down. He had noticed my pain and
struggle.

"Bernd, you stay here and eat. You are my guest."

Doron was looking at him fiercely when the others started talking.
The man sitting next to Doron reached over the table to shake my
hand.

"My name is Chaim and this fellow right next to you is Rafi and the
one next to him is Uri. We are all from Haifa. I was never in Germany.
I would like to travel there one day. I really like the cars." Chaim was a
short, muscular man with prominent cheekbones and black curly hair
that reached almost to his neck. His voice was guttural and hoarse.

"My family came from Yemen and we love to eat, so I know the look
of hunger when I see it in a person's eyes. You look hungry. Come on,
eat that." He took a round, flat pita bread and cut it open with a knife.
Then he filled it with a brownish cream, stuffed it with small pieces of
tomatoes, cucumber, salad and other vegetables I could not identify,
and topped it with a greenish paste. He handed me the bulging pita
covered by a thin paper wrap.

"Eat it," he commanded.

I was too hungry to hesitate and took several big bites. It tasted
delicious and I was wolfing it down when suddenly a wave of heat
engulfed me. My face turned purple and I gasped for air.

"That's very hot stuff," I tried to say, but my words were drowned in
a sea of laughter. All five men were laughing and crying and slapping
each other on the back.

After the laughter died down Chaim, who still could not get
control himself, reached over the table and held my face with his
two hands.

"Now you know what Israeli food is like," he said, falling back into
his seat laughing again. Moshe grinned and even Doron smiled, at
my expense. Rafi gave me some plain pita.

"Here," he said. "This will neutralize the crazy hot stuff that those
Yemenites make."

Rafi was a skinny man, almost bald, with thin-rimmed glasses
framing his small face. Even though he laughed along with the others
he didn't seem to appreciate the joke that was played on me.

"What is that?" I asked Chaim, gasping.

"Nothing special, just some *zhug*," he said. Uri added, grinning at me, "Zhug is a spicy condiment of small hot peppers, fresh coriander and garlic. It's a really hot meal for those who can take it." Uri was about forty years old and over six feet tall. Moshe told me that Uri was regarded as a gentle giant. His face was freckled and his hair red.

Crumbled and scarred skin covered both his lower arms. I later learned that he had been burned while trying to get out of a burning tank during the Yom Kippur war. Moshe told me that Uri never talked about his injuries and or mentions the chronic pain he suffers quietly every day.

The burning sensation in my mouth and stomach finally subsided, with the help of Rafi's plain pita. Doron handed me a glass of cold water, which I gratefully accepted as both a solution to a medical near-emergency and a gift from heaven.

"So I guess you had enough of this stuff," Moshe said. I could still hardly talk and just nodded in agreement. He understood and handed me a clean plate filled with rice, salad and small piece of meat,

"Here, this isn't spicy. You can trust me," he smiled.

I believed what he told me and ate.

Doron then asked me what I was doing in Israel

"You are not a Jew!" he said, eyeing me suspiciously.

"I want to visit a few friends I met in Germany and use the opportunity to learn more about the country," I replied. Doron shook his head and said something in Hebrew, which triggered a fierce exchange of words.

"What did I say?" I asked Moshe. "Why are they so angry?" Moshe turned toward me and said, "You have to understand that our people breathe and live history as part of our daily life. Our culture and religion are based on memories, and respect for our traditions and sufferings. For example, every year on *Tisha B'Av* we mourn the destruction of the first and second temples. The holiday derives its name from the fact that it is commemorated on the ninth day, or Tisha in Hebrew, of the Jewish month of Av. On that day both temples were destroyed – the first by the Babylonians in 586 B.C., the second by the Romans in 70 B.C. That happened two thousand years ago. Just forty years ago millions of our people were victims of the *Shoah*."

He used the Hebrew acronym Shoah for the Holocaust, which I later learned was the common term used by Israelis.

"They were the victims of the German criminal killing machine," he continued.

"We will remember this for generations, and many of us, including me, are still affected. This is a fresh wound in our people's collective memory. I am not blaming you personally for this crime against us, but you have to understand that people like Doron and me have a hard time dealing with Germans."

"I may sound naïve, but I am trying to understand. It is difficult, because as a child, nobody told me about what happened," I said.

"I have been trying for so long to find out on my own but I have much to learn."

I considered telling him about my father and mother, but pushed this thought aside. I was afraid that it might make it impossible to build any bridges of understanding and trust. In retrospect I see that this was a poor strategy, and that my attempts to conceal my families' past probably cost me more trust than it gained.

Moshe went on, giving me some more history.

"Jews from Germany and Eastern Europe, and their descendants, are called Ashkenazim. Doron and I are Ashkenazim. Jews from the Arab countries and those from the Mediterranean region are called Sephardim. In Israel, Sephardic Jews had a hard time in the beginning and blame the Ashkenazim for all their misery. They understand the impact of the Shoa on the Jewish people, but do not really identify with it." At that moment Rafi and Chaim broke into our conversation almost simultaneously.

"That's not true," Chaim protested.

"We have been prosecuted too and we understand the incredible impact that the Shoa had on all our people. But I cannot hold you personally responsible, Bernd. You seem to be a different kind of German. You are going to Israel to learn and understand. I respect that and therefore I am willing to accept you." I was moved by Chaim's emotional statement and was further moved when Rafi nodded in agreement.

Doron, who had been silent until now, then said,

"The others are right. You are different, but you must understand these memories are not shaken off easily and in fact, will never be shaken off from any of us. My parents' faces appear in my dreams every time I sleep. I hear them calling me by my name. They remind me not to forget. You have an open mind and that is good. I advise you to visit the Holocaust museum in Jerusalem. You will feel and understand what the Holocaust means for me, for us, and maybe for you. We live in the aftermath of the Shoah. Its repercussions can be felt everywhere in Israel."

He must have noticed the tears in my eyes and looked at me more softly.

"Come on, let's go to the cafeteria. I will buy the coffee and desserts."

When we stood he hugged me as if I were his younger brother or even his son. I was deeply moved, and from that moment on, spent the entire trip to Haifa with these men. It felt as though I was easing into Israeli society before I ever set foot in the Holy Land.

Before long, the ferry was approaching the Greek port of Piraeus, south of Athens. After docking we all disembarked for several hours to replenish our supplies. I followed Moshe's advice and bought bread, cheese, olives, and water from a local vendor before returning to the ship.

During the remainder of the trip we spent many hours together playing cards and laughing. On the night before our arrival to Haifa I noticed the growing excitement among my newly found friends. Doron approached me.

"Go to bed early tonight and try to get up before sunrise. You will not regret it." I didn't know why and I didn't ask I had learned to trust what he said to me.

I crawled into my sleeping bag, zipped it tight, and felt asleep almost instantly under the dark starlit Mediterranean sky.

It was still dark when Doron woke me by shaking my shoulder.

"Get up, Bernd. We will arrive soon in *Eretz Israel*." He used the biblical term to describe the entire Land of Israel, including the territories of Judea and Samaria, also known as the West Bank, and the Gaza Strip. Doron firmly believed that this land was given to the Jewish people by God with the charge to manage it responsibly and wisely. Little did I know how emotionally charged the term Eretz

Israel could be for some people in Israel and I soon learned to use the term carefully.

I slowly got up and saw the first rays of morning sun illuminate the horizon. I was astonished to see so many people on deck until I realized they were waiting not just for the sunrise, but for their first glimpse of Israel. When the holy land came into view, everybody fell silent. On the horizon, the sun was rising and we could see the coastal mountain range and Mt. Carmel bathed in orange light, along with Israel's northern port city of Haifa, located on the slopes. The view was breathtaking, and I saw tears in the eyes of many people, young and old, as we all stood on deck. Some were praying silently in their prayer shawls (*tallit*) and phylacteries (*teffilin*), the black leather straps with two boxes containing the Jews covenant with God. The men wore these wrapped around the left arm and over the head. The box containing the head-tefillin has a Hebrew symbol on the outside, and this, together with the letter formed by the knots of the two straps, make up the first letter of the Hebrew word *Shaddai*, one of the names of God. Each of the men appeared to be in an intimate conversation with God. I stepped back to watch in silent admiration. I felt myself identifying with their devotion to their Creator. Silently, I prayed with them.

I lost my sense of place and time and was startled by Doron, who was standing right next to me.

"Every time I have been privileged to experience this moment, I imagine the feelings of the first immigrants arriving from poverty-stricken and war-torn Europe. I was one of them when I arrived in April 1948 from a DP [Displaced Persons] camp in Germany. I felt more helpless and lonely than I can express to you now. I was only nineteen, but after having spent four years in Auschwitz, I felt like an old man. I was certain at the time that I had nothing to live for, or so I thought. Israel existed only in my imagination, and when I arrived in the land of our forefathers, I had no family and did not know what would be expected of me.

I remember that seeing Eretz Israel for the first time was like a dream. I almost had to pinch myself to be sure I had finally made it. It was a bittersweet victory for me. I had nobody to celebrate it with. My family was all gone by then. On my arrival, I was sent to a

Kibbutz, but it was a short-lived experience. In May 1948, the War of Independence broke out, and I was one of the many thousands of men who joined forces to fight the invading Arab armies. Even then, many of the friends I made were killed, so I was alone again. Many battles and wars followed, and I fought in almost all of them. I have few friends left, but I feel at home here in Eretz Israel. At least I can honor the name of those that have fallen for its defense."

Doron did not expect me to answer, but his monologue deeply touched me. I had heard my father use the term honor many times when describing his duty to fight for his homeland, but this was different. Doron was fighting for the survival of his people. My father fought for the sake of conquest, as a warrior behind the wrong cause. My feelings of guilt and shame were difficult to overcome. I longed to tell Doron the truth about myself and my family, but I had to learn to face my family of origin on my own before I could talk about it with others.

THE FIRST DAY

THE SHIP REACHED HAIFA harbor in the early morning. Around the harbor, buildings glowed in the sun's warm orange colors. The golden dome of the Bahai shrine on the slope of Mount Carmel magnified the reflection of the sunlight and contributed to the overwhelming welcome. Moshe, Doron, Uri, Rafi, and Chaim stood with me, observing my reactions.

"If I didn't know better," Rafi said, "I would almost believe that you were Jewish. You are as excited as anybody here. Israel is waiting for you, Bernd. Get to know it. Get to know the people. There are many things that will puzzle you. Many conflicts you need to resolve. Just let it settle in at first and observe. Deeper understanding will come in time."

"Anybody waiting for you?" Moshe asked. He must have noticed my nervousness and searching gaze once the ferry completed the docking maneuver.

"I think he is already looking forward to the Sabra," Chaim teased.

"What's a Sabra," I asked.

"Ah, now we still have time for a teaching moment," Doron exclaimed.

"Sabra is a Hebrew word, derived from *tzabar*, which is the name of the prickly pear cactus. Native Israelis are often compared to a thorny desert plant with a thick hide that conceals a sweet, softer interior."

"Especially the women," Chaim chuckled.

"Nu? Is a Sabra waiting for you or not?"

I blushed and avoided the conversation, but it was too late. All of them sensed that something was going on.

"So, who is she?" Rafi asked. Moshe added," Where did you meet her?" and Chaim mumbled, "She must really like you. But for a non-Jew, or goyim, you are okay."

I was not ready to field the avalanche of questions from my newfound friends.

It wouldn't take long for me to realize this insistence on frankness and openness was typical of the Israeli character.

Finally, after a very slow approach, the huge ferry docked. Its giant doors opened and allowed the cars, trucks, and passengers to disembark. Together we spilled out of the belly of this huge whale and before I realized it, I was standing on the land of Eretz Israel. I had finally arrived.

As I was pushed forward toward the customs checkpoint I tried to stay with my new friends. I felt lost without them and overwhelmed by the cacophony of voices with guttural sounding words. This was a controlled chaos. In Hebrew they use the word *tohu va-vohu*, to describe a confusion so great it requires a divine intervention to establish order. Fortunately, we did not have to wait for an act from above. Instead, several bulky and sweaty Israeli customs officers took charge of the situation and before I knew what was happening, I was standing in front of the customs counter.

He was middle-aged and obviously of Sephardic decent. His dark, curly hair was cut quite short but still formed waves on his head. His skin was dark brown and he was sweating profusely, either from the hot weather or the glass of steaming coffee he held in his left hand. A non-filter cigarette dangled from the corner of his mouth and piece of ash fell on the table as he stamped a passport. He barked commands in guttural Hebrew and did not conceal his annoyance at having to staff the desk so early in the morning.

When my turn came, I sheepishly handed him my green German passport, expecting a barrage of curse words or at least a nasty remark, but instead he placed the cup of coffee on the table and looked at me with a huge smile.

"You are a German! They really know how to play soccer. I love watching them play." He continued showering me with pleasantries about German soccer, glanced for a second at my passport picture, opened an empty page in my passport, and stamped it with an entry visa. He then took my hand and shook it.

"My name is Yossi and welcome to Israel." To say the least, I was surprised by this outburst of hospitality and noticed that Moshe and Doron had caught up with me and witnessed the entire encounter.

"Now you know," Moshe said. "We are crazy. One moment we are arrogant and unbearable and the next moment we are loveable and warm. Go figure."

He was right, because seconds later, by the time Moshe's turn came, the smiling Yossi had turned into a wild-eyed, cursing madman.

Behind the customs counter a thick iron door automatically opened, letting me out into the waiting area. Suddenly, I was being hugged and showered with kisses and it took me several seconds to understand that Vered had found me.

"You are finally here. You really kept your promise," she screamed, squeezing me tight. She was so beautiful, her blue eyes beaming with joy, her freckled face all smiles and framed by her long blond hair. We gazed into each other's eyes, neither knowing exactly what to do next. I kissed her on her forehead.

"Shalom," I said, "I am so glad to be here. You don't know how much it means to me."

She took my hand and pulled me away from the gate.

"Do you have luggage?" she asked.

"Only my backpack," I replied.

"Then let's go home. I have so many things to show you."

"No, wait," I pleaded," I have to say goodbye to my friends. I turned around and saw my five friends walking towards the parking lot, surrounded by women and children.

"Thank you for everything my friends," I shouted. Doron and

Moshe heard me and turned around and waved.

"Shalom, my friend," Doron exclaimed. "I will miss you." That was the last time I saw them, the five wise men who shared so much with me and guided me to the holy land. I had no time just then to be melancholy, but I still think of them, often with great affection. But now Vered was taking control and pulling me toward a waiting taxi.

"Where are we going?" I asked.

"I am taking you home to meet my parents," she replied.

At the harbor entrance she flagged down a large Mercedes with several passengers already inside.

"Come on," she demanded. "Let's get into the *sherut*."

I hesitated, because the cab was already filled with passengers, but Vered was already inside.

I learned quickly that a sherut, derived from a Hebrew word meaning "service," is a shared taxi that operates on fixed routes, picking up and dropping off people all along the way.

I quickly overcame my discomfort at being squeezed between several people in the back of the car, partly because one of them was Vered. She was holding my hand and beaming with joy.

"Look out the window and see my city," she insisted. "Isn't it beautiful, Bernd?"

The Sherut followed a scenic, meandering road up the Carmel Mountain, providing a breathtaking view of the city and its large, impressive harbor.

"Look here! That's the hotel where Sadat stayed during his visit to Haifa last month."

She referred to Egyptian President Anwar Al-Sadat stay in Haifa during his third and last visit to Israel. He and Israeli Prime Minister Menachem Begin tried to narrow their differences on a number of issues. Above all they wanted to demonstrate that the peace treaty they signed in March 1979 was still alive and being implemented by both parties. Unfortunately, Sadat paid with his life for his courageous peace gesture when he was murdered by Islamic extremists on October 6, 1981.

The sherut drove through several neighborhoods crowded with street merchants. Loud oriental music blasted out of small stores housed in old buildings. I immediately felt an attachment to this bustling life and its controlled chaos.

"What do you think?" Vered was asking.

"I feel at home," I answered simply. She turned toward me with surprise and smiled.

"How can you like that mess? Even I have problems dealing with it."

"I don't know, but something here seems familiar to me," I replied feeling the familiarity.

The sherut dropped off several passengers and Vered asked the driver to stop at a near-by street corner.

"Here we are," she said. "This is where I live." She pointed at a two-story duplex with a small pathway leading toward an entrance hidden behind a stone wall. When she knocked at the door I heard a female voice calling

"*Rak rega,* wait a minute," and in a few moments the door was opened by a small but imposing woman with a broad smiling face and blond-brown hair.

"Here you are *motek,* sweatheart," her mother said, and immediately hugged and kissed Vered.

"*Ima,* Mother, look! He finally arrived."

The woman turned to me and spoke in halting German.

"Shalom, my name is Bracha. A long time ago I learned to speak German and I haven't spoken it since my childhood. Please, enter and feel at home. We have made room for you to stay here with us."

I did not expect this hospitality and was reluctant to accept. Bracha seemed to notice my hesitancy and gently pushed me into a small apartment with one bedroom and a sparsely furnished living room. I was moved by her heartfelt welcome and hospitality.

"Let me show you your room," Bracha said. She took me by the hand and led me through the small kitchen. In the corner was a tiny storage space converted into a room, which barely held a bed and nightstand. The wall was covered with pictures featuring Vered with her friends and family.

"This is my room," Vered said, "and it will be your room for as long as you stay with us."

"Where are you going to sleep?" I asked, surprised.

"Don't worry I will sleep in my mom's bedroom and she is sleeping on the couch."

I was touched by their genuine effort to make me feel as comfortable as possible despite the inconvenience to them.

"You must be starving," Bracha said. "Sit down at the table. I prepared some food for you."

Within minutes the table was filled with steaming bowls of soup, grilled meat, hummus and tahini, dips made of chickpea and sesame seed paste. There was also fresh bread, *borekas* (pastry stuffed with cheese, spinach, or mushrooms), pita bread, dates, cheese, and fresh fruit. After the long journey I was hungry and tired and enjoyed the simple and delicious food.

"How long can you stay?" Vered asked.

"Exactly one week," I said. "I have to be back to continue my studies at the university. Her expression showed her disappointment, but she quickly recovered.

"I want to show you so many things, and we have little time. Let's go to bed early and tomorrow we'll take a trip to Tel Aviv and Haifa. I also have to go back to the army base and I want to take you there."

"I didn't know that you were in the army? Since when?"

"In Israel everybody has to serve, and I was drafted after I finished high school three months ago. The trip to Germany was my last opportunity to enjoy myself before the army. I just completed the basic training for girls and I am assigned to a Nahal unit in the Arava desert."

She anticipated my question about Nahal.

"Nahal is a Hebrew acronym for *Noar Halutzi Lohem* and means Fighting Pioneer Youth. It's a special army unit that combines military service with a specific type of civilian service, such as working for social welfare projects in neighborhoods and towns suffering from socioeconomic difficulties, acting as counselors for youth organizations, or founding and developing new agricultural settlements. I have chosen to work in a kibbutz in the Arava desert in the South, near Eilat. It's really great there. We are a small group of settlers and it makes me feel like I'm a pioneer. I will take you there and you will see and feel what I mean. Meanwhile, my commanding officer gave me a pass to visit my parents and to spend some time with you."

Her excitement and enthusiasm were obvious but I still had a difficult time imagining her as a soldier.

Bracha interrupted her.

"Vered is my only child and believe me I am very worried about her being in that kibbutz with all those men. It's a new kibbutz, right at the Jordanian border. They are guarding the desert border against intrusions by Palestinian terrorists coming from Jordan."

"Come on, Ima. It's not that dangerous. It's a quiet border and nothing has happened there in the last few years. We are building a new community and developing new farm land there. Its exciting and fun."

Bracha rolled her eyes.

"Yes, I was an idealistic Zionist once also. But over the years I have learned that you cannot live on idealism alone." She turned toward me.

"I was only sixteen years old when I arrived in Israel from Romania and I lived through the early years and struggles of our state. I married young and we settled here in Haifa. Everything was so difficult in those years. It was hard to find work and a place to live, and sometimes we ran out of food. When Vered was born, I finally found happiness and thought that everything would be fine. But then in June, 1967, the Six-Day War broke out and Vered's father vanished on the Golan Heights.We never found out what happened to him. He either was killed and his body was never found or he was caught by the Syrians and disappeared in a prison." Her face revealed the pain that she still felt. Her eyes filled with tears and Vered hugged her.

"It's okay, Ima. I am here."

"Oh Vered, I am so proud that you are in the army, but am so afraid of losing you, too."

I didn't know what to do. I was not part of the family, but her mother was openly sharing her feelings before me. How different from my family, I thought, where emotions were hidden and feelings were never discussed. I watched Bracha and Vered embracing and kissing each other with a deep emotional connection I had never experienced.

Bracha turned toward me, wiping away her tears.

"I am sorry. You are our guest and I am crying instead of

entertaining you. Tell me about yourself, Bernd. Where are your parents from? How did they survive the war?"

This was the question I feared the most. I felt ashamed of disclosing my life and was not yet able to reveal the truth. This shame led me to conceal my feelings and prevented me from being honest with others.

Vered saved me.

"Ima, I told you. Bernd is not Jewish, he is a friend of Israel and wants to learn more about us."

Bracha's eyes opened wide and slowly she came out with an even more embarrassing question.

"You are here to learn about Jews? What do your parents think about that?"

Again, I had no answer. Should I her tell her the truth about my father? Explain why I was searching for answers? What would she think if I told her everything about my father and his past?

I did my best.

"Honestly, Bracha, I don't know exactly what I am doing here. I just feel that it's something I have to do. My parents do not support what I am doing and I really do not care. I am just happy to be here and I feel honored to be your guest."

This seemed acceptable, even though I had given her only a grain of the truth. Bracha stepped closer and kissed me on my forehead.

"You have a good heart. We will take care of you. Don't you worry." At that moment I felt optimistic that I might be judged by who I was and not by the shadow cast upon me by my father.

Vered took my arm and pulled me away from her mother.

"Go to sleep Bernd. We have a long day tomorrow. *Leila tov,* Good night, my friend," and she kissed me on the cheek.

THE SECOND DAY

IT WAS STILL EARLY in the morning when Vered woke me.

"Get up my friend. We have to leave soon."

I must have slept at least ten hours, but was still drowsy because of the long journey. But it was time to get up and start my first full day in this exciting country. After shaving and showering I enjoyed the cup of strong coffee Bracha made me.

Vered was already calling to me from the door.

"Don't waste your precious time having breakfast. We will eat on the way. Hurry up, we have to catch the bus."

"Where are we going?" I asked.

"I'll tell you later. Just come."

Bracha handed me a bag of sandwiches and embraced me.

"Take care of her. She is the light of my life."

Before I could answer Vered was pulling me toward the door.

"Don't worry Ima. I will be fine and I will be back soon."

We rushed to the bus stop and just caught the bus to the central bus station in Haifa.

"Where are we going ?" I asked as we rode.

"To Tel Aviv, and from there to Jerusalem. I want to show you so many different places, but we have little time. In two days I have to report back to the army. Lets make the best of it."

I was disappointed to learn how short our time would be, but looked forward to every second of it. We caught the bus to Tel Aviv, which took us on the coastal highway.

Along the way we passed several villages that Vered pointed out.

"These are Arab villages. I mean Israeli-Arab villages. Did you know that almost twenty percent of all Israeli citizens are Palestinian Arabs?"

"Have you visited any of those villages?"

She turned toward with a surprised smile.

"No, as a woman I don't feel comfortable going there and especially now that I am serving in the army I cannot go."

"Why not?"

"For security reasons. They may abduct or hold you or whatever. I really do not want to talk about it."

I was curious and puzzled, because I noticed her ambivalent attitude toward Arabs and was determined to find out why.

"What do Israelis think about the Palestinian Arabs living in their midst?"

She frowned and hesitated for several seconds.

"You know, Bernd, I was born here. This is my country and I love it. In my short life I have witnessed two wars and my uncle was badly injured in the last one."

"You mean the one you call the Yom Kippur war. I remember it too."

"Yes, the last one was the worst. The Arabs attacked us on our holiest day. The Day of Atonement when everyone is at home or in the synagogue. On the Golan Heights and in the Sinai, our troops were almost overrun, but against all odds we held firm and fought back. You know during that time I remember Arabs in Haifa rejoicing when Syria and Egypt attacked. I always thought that they would be grateful for being able to live in Israel. No other democracy exists in the Middle East. They can vote, run for office, and even have representation in our parliament, the *Knesset*. Their children, like Chalid, whom you met in Germany, go to school and universities. They should be grateful, but I feel that they are just waiting for the right moment to stab us in the back. So, yes, I have a problem going to their villages."

"So why did you join the peace mission to Germany?"

"Because I felt it was the right thing to do, to learn more about one another. I still want to do that, but I am ambivalent about the whole issue."

She turned toward me and I noticed that her face was flushed.

"Listen, I do my best to understand them. I learned Arabic at school, I had Palestinian students in my class, I participated in that mission to Germany, and I really tried to understand them, but I always get the feeling that they don't want to understand us. It's always the same story for them. We occupied their land. We kill their brothers and sisters in the occupied territories. We discriminate against them and they are second class citizens. I sometimes have the impression that they do not want to get to know *us*."

After a moment she went on.

"I was so happy and hopeful when Sadat came to Israel in November 1977 and offered peace. But we are left with only a signed peace of paper. We need to make peace and learn to live with each other. It's so difficult and sometimes I get tired of trying." She sank back in her chair, appearing angry.

I reflected on what she said. So many lives had been lost in the wars between Israel and its Arab neighbors. So much misery and pain for so many families. Then I remembered a sentence from Anwar El-Sadat's address to the Knesset on that historic day, November 20, 1977:

"Any life that is lost in war is a human life, be it of an Arab or an Israeli. A wife who becomes a widow is a human being entitled to a happy family life, whether she be an Arab or an Israeli."

Vered and other Israelis shared this need for mutual respect and acknowledgement of the right to life for both sides. Nevertheless, the way toward peace appeared so long and hard. So many obstacles, each seeming insurmountable. It seemed to me worth trying, but who was I to expect it from my hosts?

My thoughts were interrupted when the bus entered the central bus station in Tel Aviv. As we left the bus, we were suddenly surrounded by hundreds of people hurrying toward other buses, including soldiers carrying their M-16's, or Galil assault rifles, rushing home or back to their bases. The air was filled with diesel exhaust fumes and an inferno of heat and odor rising from the hot asphalt; my senses were battered by loud oriental music blasting out of the small record shops surrounding the bus station. I felt completely lost and was glad that Vered was leading me by the hand through this man-made mess.

"Are you hungry?" Before I could answer she had stopped at one of the many falafel stands and bought us a couple.

"Take it," she said, and before I could answer she handed me a round pita. "You have to fill it with those salads." She pointed to the dozens of trays overflowing with colorful salads and vegetables, and as I hesitated she stuffed my pita with so many ingredients it resembled a small football.

"What does falafel mean?"

"Oh, it comes from the Arabic word *filfil*, meaning pepper, and we integrated it into the Hebrew language."

How ironic, I thought. Jews adopted Arabic words and cuisine, but the two peoples were so far apart. This would be a recurring experience, and I continue to ask myself why both people were so far apart, even though they had so much in common.

I quickly learned to appreciate the taste of the oriental food and spices, being careful at the same time to stay away from the fiery zhug.

Vered and I quickly finished eating and hurried to a bus operated by Egged, the largest bus company in Israel, which provides a tight network of service routes that is tying together the tiny country. The bus to Jerusalem was already filled with passengers who seemed to represent the entire spectrum of Israeli society: Religious Jews dressed in black suits and black hats; Arab women with colorful head-coverings and shawls; young and very attractive Israeli women wearing tight jeans and even tighter shirts. My obvious attraction to their presence evoked a smile from Vered.

"You seem to enjoy the scenery in Israel. Soon you won't need me to show you around."

She had caught me.

"No, no. I just looked. I mean I didn't intend to look."

She was enjoying my discomfort and obvious embarrassment.

"Come on. This is Israel. Don't hold back; enjoy yourself. I am just teasing you."

Beneath the joking, I was not at all sure what to expect from our relationship. I was torn between my strong attraction to her and the realization that I would part soon from an attractive girl who would not stay alone for long. I forced myself to purge those thoughts from my mind and tried to experience the country I was longing for.

The bus slowly freed itself from the dozens of others and merged onto the highway leading away from congested Tel Aviv. The driver was obviously experienced and skilled, but his driving style seemed better suited driving tanks than working in civilian life. He abruptly accelerated and hit the breaks as if he had no passengers. No one else seemed bothered by it, however, and I started to get used to it.

On the road to Jerusalem, we passed through the outskirts of Tel Aviv, passed the international airport, and then began a slow ascent toward the mountain slopes on which Jerusalem sits. I noticed the metallic skeletons of various vehicles scattered on the slopes along the road.

"What are those?" I asked Vered.

"Those are reminders of our War of Independence. One day after Ben Gurion declared Israel's independence on May 15, 1948, and created the State of Israel, the Arab armies of Egypt, Syria, Jordan, Iraq, Saudi Arabia, and Lebanon invaded us. We were outnumbered by their soldiers, who also had more modern weapons. Against all odds we prevailed, but the bloody battle of Latrun, for access to Jerusalem, was fought here. We want to preserve the memory of those brave men and women who lost their lives, and the jeeps and tanks left behind on the battlefield are maintained as a permanent reminder of their sacrifice."

Before I had time to speak she pointed out a large, castle-like structure on a hilly ridge surrounded by vineyards.

"Look, that's the Latrun monastery. Isn't it beautiful?"

"What is it about? Who built it?"

"Well, as far as I know it was built by French monks on the ruins of an old crusader castle, and they still produce great wine and fantastic cheese there. This area also has great significance in Jewish history. It is called the Ayalon valley where, according to the Bible, Joshua defeated the Amorites. It was also the scene of many battles for access to Jerusalem during the Crusades, just like the battles in our 1948 war of independence. The Latrun fort was built by the British army as a police station and later taken by the Jordanians until we recaptured it during the Six-Day War in 1967. Now we use it as a military museum, and soldiers are honored and sworn in here. By the way, right next to it on and around that hilltop is the village of Neve Shalom. You remember – that's the reason we came to Germany. It's a village that was founded by Bruno Hussar, a Jew who converted to Christianity and who believes that Jews and Muslims can only find peace if they learn to live together."

"What does Neve Shalom mean?" I asked.

"Literally translated it means the Oasis of Peace. Bruno, together with Elias, whom you met in Germany, started those trips to Germany where young Jews and Arabs can teach each other about their respective cultures."

"Do you believe in that?" I asked her directly.

She stared out of the window and shrugged her shoulders.

"I don't know. Sometimes I want to believe in it and sometimes I get angry when I hear about terror attacks and random killings of Jews. I go to school with Israeli Arabs and I want to believe that they are different. Who knows."

Her short lecture was filled with violence, warfare, and also hope.

What bothered me was her casual narration of the events surrounding this place.

"Do you think about all the people who were killed here?" I asked.

"Oh yes, I do. One of my relatives was killed here during the War of Independence. But that's life here in Israel. We always have to struggle here not only for our freedom but to continue to survive."

That sounded similar to my father's stories of the wars he, his father and grandfathers fought for Germany. I remembered that he took the entire family for a trip to France – not to visit Paris or the sunny beaches of the Cote d'Azur, but the battlefields of Verdun, the site of the longest and bloodiest battles of the First World War. One million invading German troops fought two hundred thousand French defenders. Casualties were estimated at almost one million soldiers, half of them being fatalities. Despite the slaughter on both sides and the massive loss of human life, neither side gained tactical or strategic advantage. In the midst of the now barren and empty battlefields, only the scattered stone memorials engraved with thousands of names serve as silent reminders of the carnage. The piercing screams of the wounded have been carried away by the cold wind, and the blood-drenched earth with its hundreds of mass graves is now fertile farmland.

My father stopped at each memorial, searching for a name, and finally he found what he was looking for. I remember his pained expression when he carefully touched the engraved name. He took my hand and pulled me toward the memorial. With a trembling voice he slowly pronounced the name. "First Lieutenant G-u-e-n-t-h-e-r W-o-l-l-s-c-h-l-a-e-g-e-r." This was my father's uncle, though I had never met him. He fell in battle on February 22, 1916, leading his soldiers into the fight. My father said that he was last seen with his sword held high, leaping from a trench and calling upon his troops to follow him. He was the first to die in a hail of bullets.

My father's eyes filled with tears and he stopped talking. I never saw him so emotional, and I tried to hug and comfort him. He pushed me away and looked at me fiercely.

"Listen," he hissed at me, "wars have to be fought and men have to die for the honor of our country. Nobody respects this anymore.

No one understands us anymore. I was a soldier and an officer and I was willing to sacrifice myself. I wish I had succeeded."

I was hurt by his outburst of anger and frustration, but was too young then to understand. I knew that if he had died, I would have had no father. This, I thought, was a father who preferred to die for his country than to care for his only son. This experience opened the first fissure in my relationship with him. I swore to myself that I would never be like him, fighting and wishing to die for something.

"Are you day-dreaming?" Vered was shaking my shoulder.

"No, no," I lied, trying to regain my composure.

"Come on, lets not think about the past. We have almost reached Jerusalem. Let's enjoy ourselves."

Jerusalem, the magical city, was almost in sight. Suddenly I saw a sign indicating the exit to Abu Gosh, the Arab village where my new friend Chalid lived.

"Shall we get out here and visit Chalid?" I asked excitedly.

She looked at me as if I were mad.

"I really do not want to do that. Didn't I tell you that as a woman I feel very uncomfortable around those Arab guys?"

"But you also told me that you tried to understand Arabs and live in peace with them."

"But going to school with them and visiting them in their village is different," she responded angrily.

"You can visit him and send him my best regards."

I could see I would have to drop the topic, slowly coming to terms with this reality that it would be difficult to balance the two worlds my new friends lived in – different lives in the same society. It was not a formula for peace and understanding, but then, here I was, a German whom some Jews eyed suspiciously and some Arabs saw as the representative of a people who "succeeded" in killing the Jews.

The sight of Jerusalem on the horizon brought an opportunity to change the topic of our conversation. Bright sunlight highlighted the yellowish, almost golden color of the walls around Jerusalem.

"I love this city," Vered exclaimed.

"Did you know that until 1967 Jews could not enter the old city? Now we can enter and visit as we please. You will see how marvelous and wonderful it is."

We arrived a the busy and crowded bus station. Hundreds of armed male and female soldiers were changing buses or waiting for rides to the army bases around Jerusalem or in the occupied territories. They all seemed relaxed and walked with pride, their loaded automatic weapons dangling from their shoulders. I could see that the few Arabs in the crowd were not at all relaxed, but seemed tense and angry.

"Tell me Vered, does everyone here serve in the army?"

"Yes of course," she replied quickly, looking at me curiously.

"All Israeli citizens serve in the military after the completion of their high school education."

"And what about your Arab citizens? Young men such as Chalid? What are they doing after their graduation?"

She obviously felt uncomfortable answering the question.

"You know it's true that they are Israeli citizens, but we really don't allow them to serve in the Army because we do not want them to be in a situation where we have to rely on them fighting other Arabs."

"But I have heard that Druze and Bedouins serve in the Army."

"They are different," she almost snapped at me angrily.

"They are willing to serve and even asked to serve voluntarily to demonstrate their loyalty. Did you know that in those villages where Muslims and Druze live together, they often fight because the Druze send their sons into the army."

I had touched yet another raw nerve. So many conflicts, contradictions, and disagreements in such a small country.

"Come on, Bernd. We have little time and so much to see. Let me show you some of the magnificent sites. But first we need to stop at a place which is important for me and for you to see."

"What is it?" I asked curiously.

She gave me a serious and sad look.

"We are going back in the past to witness and to learn so that history won't repeat itself. I will show you *Yad Vashem.*"

Despite the heat of the midday sun I felt a cold shiver down my spine. Yad Vashem, the place and name for those millions of victims who were not given the dignity of a Jewish burial, or any burial at all. Yad Vashem, Israel's official memorial site for the victims of the Holocaust. Yad Vashem, a place made necessary by my father's generation's crimes against humanity. The closer the bus came to the gates of this memorial, the sicker I felt. I did not know what to expect and Vered sensed my fear and tension. She took my hand and pressed it gently but firmly, looking at me with her beautiful eyes.

"I can only imagine how you feel now. I don't take you here to make you feel bad. It's an important place for me and my family, because my mother lost almost her entire family in the Shoa. Their ashes were scattered somewhere in Poland. For me this place is the only place where I can mourn and honor them."

The bus stropped at the gate of the Holocaust memorial located on *Har Hazikaron,* the Hill of Remembrance, a ridge on the western outskirts of Jerusalem. All the passengers got off the bus slowly and silently.

We walked along an alley between rows of trees.

"These are trees planted in honor of those brave men and women who risked themselves to save Jews during the Shoa. We call them 'Righteous Among the Nations' and honor them here. There are more than twenty thousand names."

I was stunned. So many trees, each of them representing a courageous person. Most if not all of them were non-Jews who saved Jewish lives. One plaque in a small garden caught my eye because of the German name: Wilm Hosenfeld. I later found out that he was a German army officer and a member of the Nazi party who felt ashamed of what was done to the Jews in the name of his country and tried to help as best as he could. He was captured by Soviet soldiers in 1945, sent to a prison camp, and died there. I wondered if my father would have been capable of such behavior. Why did he ignore the unspeakable suffering? Why did he continue to avoid this issue, which split us apart?

Vered was still holding my hand and leading me toward a building that looked like a cathedral with a low, tent-like roof.

"This is the memorial chamber," she whispered into my ear.

Through a corridor we entered a large hall illuminated by torches affixed to the wall. Engraved in the black basalt floor were the names of dozens of concentration camps and mass killing sites in Central and Eastern Europe: Auschwitz, Majdanek, Buchenwald, Dachau, Birkenau, Sobibor, Treblinka, Chelmno, Belzek. I had to stop reading as each name seemed to pierce my eyes. More then six million men, women, and children. Six million hopes and lives. And what was left? A small crypt in front of the memorial flame containing some ashes of victims. I sank to my knees, bent my head in shame, and started to cry. For the first time I felt the physical pain of grief and loss. Vered knelt next to me and embraced me.

Our faces, both washed in tears, touched each other, I sobbed.

"I am so sorry. I am so sorry." That was all I could say before my voice was drowned by my tears. We held each other for what felt like an eternity, but was probably just a few minutes.

The son of a perpetrator and the daughter of a survivor, crying together, trying to help and support each other. I finally had the strength to get up and she looked into my teary eyes.

"You are not responsible for what happened, Bernd," she said. "I feel that there are things that you don't want to share with me, because you are ashamed. But you will. Eventually you will. You are different, very different, from those who committed those crimes. You seek the truth to heal yourself. I am proud that you had the courage to come here. I am proud to be here with you. Let's leave this place, but not forget. Never forget! Let me show you something else."

We left the memorial hall through a corridor lined with dozens of pictures illuminated by bright sunlight coming through the Plexiglas roof.. They were all aerial photographs taken by Allied bombers during the Second World War. Some were of Auschwitz and Birkenau, indicating that the Allies knew the location of these camps and indeed successfully undertook several bombing campaigns in their vicinity. On August 20, 1944, a fleet of U.S. bombers dropped more than one thousand bombs on the factory areas of Auschwitz, some less than five miles from the gas chambers. On September 13, American bombers struck the factory areas again; this time stray bombs accidentally hit an SS barracks, killing fifteen Germans; a slave labor workshop, killing forty prisoners; and the railroad track leading to the gas chambers. The frequent Allied bombings of seven other synthetic oil refineries near Auschwitz during 1944 and 1945 included a January 20 raid on Blechhammer, forty-five miles from the death camp, which made it possible for forty-two Jewish slave laborers to escape.

Vered pointed angrily at the pictures.

"You see? They knew about it, but they chose not to do anything. They should have bombed the gas chambers."

"How do you know that they knew what was going on in the camps? On the pictures you cannot see anything except the barracks and the factory buildings."

"They knew, Bernd, "she replied firmly.

"Several prisoners escaped and were debriefed by American and British intelligence agents who heard and recorded the stories but chose not to believe them. They either knew or refused to believe that Germans or anybody else would be capable of committing systematic mass murder."

Her words reminded me of my father's behavior. Nothing like that could have taken place. A war should be fought with honor, for the ideals of the fatherland. He closed his eyes and ears to anything different. He led his tank unit into battle and conquered land that latter was drenched with the blood and covered by the ashes of so many innocent victims. Now I understood why Israel built this memorial and why every year an entire day is dedicated to the memory of those who perished in the Shoa. Never forget! Remember what happened or we will repeat past mistakes.

"Come on, Bernd. We have to hurry if I'm going to show you Jerusalem."

It was already late afternoon, and we planned to catch a bus to the south of the country, back to her army unit. We took the bus to the Old City of Jerusalem and finally arrived at the Jaffa Gate, which is one of the eight stone portals granting access through the Old City walls. The name is derived from the road that lead in ancient times to the port city of Jaffa, near modern Tel Aviv. Through the gate one can access the Christian, Armenian, Muslim, and Jewish quarters.

Immediately after entering the city I was surrounded by dozens of vendors offering their goods. Cars pushed their way through the narrow road leading along the inside of the wall through the Armenian quarter. I watched as a young man sitting on a donkey packed with bags of potatoes and firewood skillfully crisscrossed his way up the street. The air was filled with the aromas of freshly brewed Arab coffee and dozens of spices. Arab music blasted out of every small store, and people pushed each other along in their hurry. My senses were once again overwhelmed by this dazzling sounds, smells, and sights of Israel.

Vered again took my hand recognizing that I was feeling lost and overwhelmed. Just south of the Gate we saw the Citadel of Jerusalem with the Tower of David, and next to it an Armenian monastery. She was heading toward a narrow pathway leading though the Muslim quarter. Along this pathway hundreds of little stores offered everything from cheap souvenirs to pricey jewelry. The store vendors swarmed around me, trying to lure me into their stores, but Vered's stern look served to keep them at bay.

"Why are you are so serious?" I asked.

"I just don't like them getting so close and pulling my arm or clothes to get me into their store. They don't respect me. I am just a woman for them."

The pathway suddenly ended and we turned right toward the Jewish quarter. Its apartments, synagogues, and stores were all built according to prevailing building codes, which mandated that all buildings be covered with native Jerusalem stone.

"Before the Six-Day War, no Jews were allowed lo live in this part of Jerusalem," Vered said, once again angry.

"The Jordanians desecrated the Jewish places of worship and used the tombstones from Jewish cemeteries to pave the roads. Jews were not even allowed to access the Western Wall, or *HaKotel*, to pray."

"But today Jews live and obviously thrive in this part of the city. I don't see any wall that separates Jews from Arabs, and we can feely pass from an section to the next."

"That's because we are stronger and they don't dare to bother us anymore," she answered.

Fear and strength seemed to trump mutual respect and understanding in this tiny land. I began to look forward to experiencing a different perspective on this conflict that smoldered in the midst of a society I was learning to admire. The country and its contradictions that fascinated me.

She was walking toward a stairwell that led to a small pathway between a array of tightly built small apartments, and suddenly we entered a large open space. Before us was the Western Wall itself.

In my readings I had learned that the Wall is part of the holiest site in Judaism, the Temple Mount, where the first and second Jerusalem temples were built. The Divine Presence is said to rest upon the top of the Temple Mount, and the gate of heaven directly above that.

The Dome of the Rocks, also called Al-Aqsa Mosque, was built by an Islamic ruler in the 6th century on the top of the former Temple Mount and is one of the three sacred sites in the Muslim faith. Its gold-overlaid dome is a distinguished landmark that dominates the view of Jerusalem. The rock over which it is built is sacred to both Muslims and Jews. In Islam, the Prophet Muhammad is believed to have ascended into heaven from the site and in Judaism it is the site where Abraham prepared to sacrifice his son Isaac. I wondered how two cultures whose faith shared similar origins could be engaged in such a bitter feud.

The Western Wall, called *Ha Kotel Ha'Maariv* in Hebrew, is the remnant of the Second Temple, torn down by the Romans in 70 A.D. According to legend, the Romans left the wall standing as a bitter reminder of the Jews' disobedience. Ever since then the Jews have mourned and wailed at the site, although the term "Wailing Wall" is controversial. Many people reject it as derogatory and inappropriate, because prayer and not self-pity should be the focus there.

According to the faithful, Jews' thrice-daily prayers may help to reconcile *Am Israel*, the people of Israel, with their God. In response, God will bring the exiled Jews back to Israel and build the Third Temple signifying the beginning of the messianic era.

The large square was filled with people trying to pray and with curious tourists who looked much like us. Hundreds of religious Jews engaged in fervent prayers at the Wall itself, touching the rock with their hands and foreheads.

"Let's go to the Wall and leave a note," said Vered, pulling me forward. "It will bring us luck."

"Why a note?" I asked.

"It's a tradition to place a prayer written on a small piece of paper in a crack in the Wall. People write all kinds of stuff, asking for health, luck, love, riches."

A fence prevented direct access to the Wall and another fence divided the areas of prayer for men and women.

"You have to go to the other side of the wall," Vered said. "The religious Jews don't allow men and women to mingle together in prayer. I guess they are afraid that women as beautiful as I am will distract others from prayer," she said, laughing.

"I would get distracted," I said, blushing as she smiled at me.

I was unsure about entering the area close to the Western Wall. I was not Jewish and did not want to interfere with those who were praying. Their devotion was obvious as they rocked their upper torsos forward and backward, either in silence or loudly reciting prayers. Finally I gathered my courage and approached the small gate. A security guard handed me a small skullcap, or *Kippa*, which I placed on my head for the first time ever. After a few steps, which seemed to take an eternity, I stood in front of the Wall itself. The huge rectangular stones appeared to have been set perfectly in place, and I saw that the cracks between them were indeed filled with small rolled paper notes.

Suddenly I remembered my mother's wish to write a prayer on her behalf and to slip it in between these stones.

Faithfully, I followed my mother's request. After doing so I closed my eyes to pray for her soul. I forgot the world around me and imagined the thousands of people who had prayed at this very spot over the centuries. I could almost hear their voices and whispered prayers, feel their presence and the rhythmic movement of their bodies. Suddenly my body was moving with them, my mind finding words of prayer, my hands touching the wall to feel its spiritual energy.

I lost my sense of time and place and prayed with a fervor I had never felt before. I was weeping and I felt the divine presence in me. I became one with the those who prayed around me.

Slowly I returned to the world around me, turned, and was about to leave the area next to the wall when I was approached by an old man with a gray beard, dark hat and black suit.

"*Shalom aleichem*," he said in Hebrew, but quickly switched to English when he saw that I did not understand him.

"I noticed you praying. What is your name and where are you from?" he asked.

I hesitated, fearing that my reply would anger him. I still felt that some would consider the presence of a non-Jew an intrusion on their personal and intimate religious life.

"I am from Germany," I answered cautiously.

"There are still Jews in Germany after all that happened?" he asked.

"I guess there are. But I am not one of them. My name is Bernd and I am sorry that I bothered you." I decided I had to escape from this uncomfortable situation.

He stepped closer to me, grabbed my hand and looked into my eyes. I saw, or imagined I saw, surprise, curiosity, and wisdom, and I felt drawn to him.

"I watched you pray," he said. "Only a Jew would pray like that. If you are not a Jew, as you say, you may have the soul of a Jew." He closed his eyes and pressed my hand against his heart.

"A lonely *Neschama* seeking a home may have found you and you are carrying this neschama with you without knowing."

"What is a neschama?" I asked.

"Ah, my young friend," and he opened his eyes widely and laughed. "The Kabbala teaches us that the human soul has several levels. At the core of our being we have a neshama, which is always connected to the Divine Presence. It is difficult to tell where the divine presence ends and the person begins. This neshama is connected to our *ruach*, our spiritual being,which in turn is connected to our *nefesh*, the life force that burns within us and is the engine that drives us. We humans are always living in a conflict between raw life forces, our nefesh, and the awareness of our spirituality, our ruach, and this conflict creates within us a confusion as to who and what we are. This conflict is the source of our sins and transgressions, and is the dilemma that forms the backdrop against which we exercise our free will. Reaching the level of neschama is the highest level of spirituality. Often we do not know that we have the neschama within us. You don't know, but you came here to find it. You were driven by an unknown force to find it. Therefore you are here. Therefore we met. Therefore I talk to you to raise your awareness."

I was speechless. This man seemed to open the door to my inner being and suddenly I realized I was here for a purpose: I was searching, not only searching for answers about my father's past, but also about myself.

"Tell me, who are you?" I asked.

He let go of my hand and stepped back.

"That's not important. Don't ask about me. Find the answers for yourself. Seek and you will find." He turned and before I knew it, he had disappeared into the crowd of Orthodox men who all wore the same black outfit and black hat. Who was he? Why did he approach me?

I was drifting through the gate in a dreamlike state when Vered touched my shoulder.

"What happened to you? You were gone for ages. What were you talking with the Dossi? Be careful. They only want money. They don't work, but have to feed a large family."

"What is a Dossi?" I asked.

"That's what we call the religious people. They tell us how we should live our lives. Not to drive a car on Shabbat, whom to marry, and so on. They don't serve in the Army, but we have to defend them. I really don't like them."

Something else for me to learn about: the level of animosity among Jews. I knew about the simmering conflict between the Ashkenazi Jews and the Sephardim, but until now I knew little about the animosities between secular and religious Israelis.

"Actually, he did not want money. He just wanted to talk to me."

"About what?" she asked.

"He talked about the neschama."

She laughed and pinched my chest.

"Wake up! You are falling for this *Kabbala* gibberish. I can't believe it. I thought you were an intelligent guy."

I felt angry and embarrassed at the same time and tried to understand her reaction.

"What's the problem with that? And what does Kabbala mean?"

"Actually, I am not the expert, but as far as I remember from my mandatory and boring religious classes at high school, Kabbala is a Jewish form of mysticism. It deals with God, the fate of human beings, and their souls, and all of that is hidden behind a veil of secrecy. But why bother with all this stuff. Let's have fun!"

I knew that further questioning would be useless, but made a mental note to ask others about Kabbala.

She pointed toward the wall surrounding Jerusalem.

"Lets go watch the sunset," she said. We left the Western Wall behind us and the mysterious Jewish wise man who had touched my heart and soul, and who had opened the gate to my identity.

A grand wall built by an Ottoman ruler in 1556, and only interrupted by eight gates, surrounds Jerusalem's Old City. We climbed the stairs from the Jaffa gate toward the Western Wall and walked along a small path that brought us a breathtaking view of the valley below.

"Let's sit down," she said. "Do you see the village in the valley and the houses along the slopes? This is an Arab village and farther on the horizon you can see the outskirts of Bethlehem. For a Christian like you, it's of great significance because it's the birthplace of Jesus, and for us Jews, too. Rachel's tomb is right outside the city of Bethlehem."

"Why do you assume that I am a Christian?" I asked.

She looked at me, perplexed. "But you were born in Germany. I assumed that you must be Christian."

"Well, I was baptized, and on my birth certificate I am listed as a Catholic, but I never practiced that religion, and honestly I am confused about where I belong."

"Why do you sound so angry and defensive?" she asked.

"Maybe because I do not really know why I am here in Israel. Initially, I came to seek answers for all the questions I asked in Germany about the *Shoa*, the crimes committed by Germans against your people, and of course the role my father played during that dreadful part of German history. Now I feel that there are other issues I need to explore. Why am I so attracted to this country? Why do I feel at home here? Why does Jewish faith and prayer seem to touch something deep inside me? Now I am searching for who I am, and since we have been here in Jerusalem, I have felt so close to finding it, but I still don't know."

"Is that the reason that you were speaking with the religious guy?"

"I guess that's one of the reasons." I did not feel comfortable telling her about my spiritual experience. I gathered from her attitude that she wouldn't understand.

"Well, anyway, whoever you are or whatever you want to be, it's up to you. I just hope you can come to terms with yourself and find your happiness." She smiled and gave me a hug. "Lets just watch the sunset."

We sat in silence watching the valley, the houses along the slopes and the city of Bethlehem in an orange glow. The voice of a Muezzin issued the call to prayer. In the background, bells were ringing, and when we turned we could still see Jews praying at the Western Wall. Spiritual practice was going on simultaneously in three faiths.

Jerusalem symbolizes the confluence of three major world religions, and at this very moment, harmony prevailed. But I had experienced the animosities and frictions between the cultures and knew that I had to expect more.

Our time was running out and we had to move quickly once again. We extracted ourselves from this eternal movement of harmony and tranquility and hurried towards the bus that would take us to the central bus station. Ahead of us lay the night ride to the south of Israel. Our final destination was a small and relatively new kibbutz, or collective community, called Yahel, in the Arava valley just forty miles north of Eilat. Eilat is Israel's southernmost city, located on the Gulf of Eilat and just across from the Jordanian port city of Aqaba.

Just in time, we boarded the bus. It was filled to the last seat with tourists traveling to Eilat, soldiers on their way to their units in the South, and those who were returning to the kibbutzim and *moshavim* or cooperative agriculture communities in the desert. Vered was serving in a Nahal unit attached to the kibbutz, which was situated just along the border of Jordan. It required military protection against the constant threat of Palestinian terrorists, who had attempted to infiltrate that area since the founding of Israel in 1948.

It was already dark when the bus left Jerusalem and Vered and I were exhausted from the day's events. We both needed a restful sleep and I was doubtful that we could do that in a bus.

Vered looked at me.

"You are as tired as I am. Let's sleep." She placed her head on my shoulder and wrapped her arms around me.

"Good night, my confused friend," she mumbled.

"Good night my excellent tour guide," I replied. The rhythmic movement of the bus and her soft and warm body pressed against me allowed me to gently drift into a deep sleep.

THE THIRD DAY

I WAS AWAKENED BY bright sunlight shining into my eyes. I must have slept at least six hours. I felt rested and energized. Out the window, I saw nothing but rugged desert terrain with scattered, dried trees and bushes and on the horizon, the outline of a mountain ridge.

Vered was slowly opening her eyes.

"*Boker tov,* my friend," she said, yawning.

"Good morning my flower," I replied, and she greeted me with a big smile.

"People might almost think we are a couple."

"Well," I said, "the guys sitting behind us seem to think so," and I pointed to two young Israeli soldiers grinning and joking in Hebrew.

"Don't pay attention to them. Israeli guys are known for their crude humor. It's all talk. Anyway, I am hungry and thirsty and I am almost sure that a gas stop is coming up."

Sure enough, several minutes later the bus turned into a gas station along the Arava desert highway and all the passengers eagerly left the bus.

"Smell the fresh and dry desert air," Vered said, breathing deeply. "It's so different from the congested cities up north. I love the desert and I promise you will, too."

She was right. The desert had a magic attraction, but I didn't anticipate the chilly morning breeze. I expected intense dry heat.

"Why is it so chilly?" I asked.

"Because we are not in the tropics. The desert does not store the heat. At night it can be very cold and during the day the sun will boil the asphalt of the street. You will get used to it."

Half an hour later we continued our journey, now wide awake and refreshed.

"Look to your left, Bernd. That's Jordan. We are just a few hundred feet away from the border fence. Its just simple barbed wire. For many years we have had a peaceful relationship with Jordan, thanks to its king, who has secretly visited Jerusalem to meet with our leaders. Soon we will have peace with Jordan and then we can travel there together."

She was correct. Many years later, after bloodshed, death, pain, and violence, Jordan did sign a peace treaty with Israel. In retrospect I wonder if her youthful enthusiasm about peace with Israel's neighbors was shared by other Israelis too.

After more then an hour the bus came to a stop somewhere in the desert.

"That's our stop," Vered said. "Let's go."

"Go where?" I asked incredulously.

I only saw a small dirt road fading away from the main highway toward desert dunes.

"The kibbutz is near the dunes. It's about thirty minutes' walk, but we may be lucky and catch a ride."

We grabbed our backpacks, climbed down from the bus, and started walking.

"Listen, Bernd, when somebody asks you who you are, don't start by telling them that you are from Germany. A Nahal unit is attached to the kibbutz, so some sections are a military compound, where theoretically you wouldn't be allowed to enter. Just tell them you are my Jewish cousin visiting from Europe."

I felt uncomfortable, but agreed to play along in order to stay with her, wherever she went.

"Okay, I will do it, but you should have told me before. I will do my best to fit in." She smiled and gave me a kiss on the cheek.

After we had walked for about twenty minutes, I was sweating. Fortunately the sweat evaporated quickly in the dry air, but still I rejoiced when I heard the sound of an approaching car. A small, battered, dust-covered pick-up truck stopped beside us and a young man in this twenties waved his right hand.

"Shalom, *motik*, sweetheart," he said, referring to Vered in typical Israeli macho fashion.

"What are you doing here alone in the desert?" he asked, ignoring my presence.

She gave him an angry look and snapped back.

"I am from the Nahal unit and we are going back to the kibbutz."

"Oh yes, you are the new one. Fresh meat for the troops," he laughed.

Her furious look seemed to take some of the bluster out of his tone, and he waved us to the back.

"Come on, I was just joking. We don't take things too seriously here. Life is hard enough as it is."

We climbed into the back of the pick up truck and he took us straight to the kibbutz, which was fairly new and consisted of prefabricated houses surrounding a community pool and dining room. I was surprised to see how much it resembled an oasis in midst of this barren desert, with palm trees, green grass, and flower bushes.

We were greeted by a young, muscular man in military fatigues and an open khaki shirt.

"Stick to our story," Vered whispered in my ear. "This is Ariel, the local nahal commander, and he will be suspicious about you."

Indeed, Ariel was already eyeing me from afar and asked Vered something in Hebrew. He quickly approached me with an outstretched hand and a thin smile.

"So, you are the cousin from Europe," he said. "I understand that you want to make aliyah to Israel."

My blank look revealed my ignorance.

"Aliyah means immigrating to Israel, to live here," he added. So Vered had really exaggerated the reason for my visit to convince Ariel that I needed to know more about a kibbutz and Nahal. She didn't know it then, but she was more or less correct. Neither of us knew it then, but seven years later I would do exactly that and settle in Israel.

After catching Vered's pleading look, I played along with the story and nodded.

"Yes, that's right I want to make aliyah and learn more about Israel."

My answer seemed to please him and with a wide grin he placed his arm around my shoulders.

"Let me show you what we are doing here. It's nine-thirty in the morning and we were just getting ready to return to the fields after our breakfast break." I learned that living and working in this kibbutz meant getting up in the wee hours of the morning to work in the fields to avoid the blistering midday heat.

"Can you grow anything here?" I asked.

Vered and Ariel smiled at each other.

"Get ready for a big surprise," Ariel said.

"Let me show you first where you are going to stay," Vered said, and took me to a building that looked like a cargo container with windows. I saw a sparsely furnished room with a bed, chair, and table, a small adjacent bathroom, and a kitchenette.

"That's my place and you are going to stay here. There are a few old working clothes and shoes in the bathroom. I will leave you alone. Get ready quickly to join us in the fields."

Even though I had been told that Israeli women were direct and straightforward, I felt slightly uneasy at sharing this room with her. But I shook off those thoughts and tried to focus on the little time we had left together. I knew that I had to return soon to Haifa to catch the boat back to Europe and I was already trying to cope with the pain of leaving her. I had to admit that we had sensed a deep emotional bond, but had no time left to develop it.

I changed into the oversized trousers, long-sleeved shirt, and bush hat, and finished just in time to joined them outside. The early sun was already hot and I began to perspire without even moving.

Ariel was standing next to a military jeep with a large antenna mounted on its back. A Galil assault rifle hung around his right shoulder, a bullet-filled magazine protruding from the side.

"Bernd, that's your name? Correct?" he asked.

Without waiting for my answer he continued.

"Our fields are located along the Jordanian border and we had several terrorist invasions over the last few months. Most of the time the terrorists just test our response and retreat, but it can be dangerous. Several of us are armed and will patrol the fields so that you can work. Can you handle that?"

I nodded.

"Another enemy is the sun and the heat. You MUST drink at least a whole bottle of water each hour, and I will monitor you. Many people underestimate their fluid requirement and dehydrate quickly in the dry desert heat."

Ariel outlined some other rules and several minutes later Vered and I were bumping along a road toward the fields in the back of a pickup truck along with several other young members of the kibbutz. Ten minutes later we approached lush green fields where the kibbutzniks were cultivating a variety of crops, including dates, pomelos, onions, melons, watermelons, and peppers.

"How can all that flourish here in the desert?" I asked Vered.

"You just need water. Even a few drops at a time can make the difference here. The desert sand is full of minerals, but the water is as precious for our economy as oil is for yours. We try to minimize water use and limit any run-off. To do that we use drip irrigation tubing buried in the shallow sand. The buried system is protected against infiltration by tiny roots by a special material called Tarplan. Air valves open when the water is turned off and allow air into the pipe. That prevents external dirt from being sucked into the dripper. We have different types of drippers, and once we have arranged the drip irrigation lines we plant directly next to them so that the plant roots receive a constant supply of small drops – just enough to allow them to grow."

I noticed her excitement as she described the details of the agricultural projects.

"The fertile soil and the year-round sunshine allow us to harvest two to three times a year. We are so successful that we are already making a small profit. To see what the desert looks like without drip irrigation, just look across the border. The Arabs don't know how to handle agriculture."

Again, I was surprised to hear her disdain for Arabs.

"If Israel is so successful in its agricultural performance and research," I asked, "why not export your know-how to these Arab countries? Such an exchange might help promote peace and understanding."

"Actually," she said, "this is part of our peace treaty with Egypt. We'll see how it will work out."

Years later, I learned that such knowledge-export projects were actually launched. One was called the Cooperative Arid Land Agricultural Research Program, but it fizzled either from lack of sufficient funding or the ambivalent attitude of the Egyptian government towards bilateral cooperation with Israel.

Now Vered was walking toward a barren field of rocks and sand where shallow, narrow trenches ran parallel to one another for several hundred yards. In the trenches I could see that thin black plastic tubing had already been placed.

"Lets go to work!" she exclaimed.

"What do we have to do?"

"We have to carefully cover the plastic tubing with soil. Later we will plant tomatoes and watermelon seeds. With the right balance of soil and humidity we sometimes can have two harvests a year."

"I noticed that several fields are marked off for agriculture, but they are not being used."

"Well, I am not an expert in Jewish law, but I know that every seventh year of using a field it should rest for at least a year to recover. There are laws in the Torah that command us to do so. The call it the Shemitah Year, or the Land's Shabbat."

Shrugging her shoulders, she said,

"Even for a non-observant Jew like me, it makes sense because we do not want to drain all the nutrients from the soil. The founders of this kibbutz actually belong to the reform movement, but even they insist on following the tradition. Therefore we are always rotating a few extra fields for this purpose."

I realized how interwoven were Jewish culture and religion if even secular Jews like Vered accepted the dictates of religion in their agricultural work.

We finally got to work. After a short while I noticed that the actual labor was not physically demanding, but the blistering heat made it difficult to work for longer than about thirty minutes.

"Don't forget to drink plenty of water."

I was happy to comply, and enjoyed every sip of the cold fresh water from the huge yellow water containers placed along the field. We worked silently for almost five hours, and finally Ariel returned to pick us up with his jeep. I was covered with sandy dust and my face was baked by the sun.

"I see that you guys had fun," he teased me. "Lets go back to the kibbutz. It's enough for one day and I guess you are hungry and tired."

At the kibbutz I took a long and welcome shower and changed into clean clothes while Vered waited for me. Silently she watched me change and then she undressed and walked into the bathroom for her own shower.

"Don't wait for me," she shouted above the noise of the water. "Just go to dining room and start eating."

"Should I save you a seat?"

She laughed and peaked out.

"This is not a restaurant in Germany. We are very informal and just want to get together and eat. Sit wherever you want. We will meet there."

Once I entered the large dining room, I saw what she meant. Several dozen young kibbutzniks and soldiers were sitting at several long tables, eating and talking loudly. Ariel saw me and waved his hand.

"Grab some food and sit here." He pointed toward the row of food trays filled with a variety of meat and dairy dishes – indicating that the Jewish dietary laws, also called Kashrut, which mandate a separation of meat and dairy dishes, were not being followed in this kibbutz. After getting my food, I sat down at his table next to another muscular soldier with long curly hair.

"Meet Avner," Ariel said.

"Avner, Bernd is one of Vered's relatives from Europe and he is interested living in Israel."

Avner nodded his head silently and continued eating.

"Avner is not a man of many words, but of action. He is responsible for the border fence security. As you probably have seen today the fence cannot keep the terrorists away from our fields. Avner works with local Bedouins to catch them."

"I never heard about Bedouins working with the army."

Avner broke his silence.

"Local Bedouin tribes have lived here in the desert and in the Negev for hundreds of years. They are still nomads and often refuse to settle down. Their men are expert trackers and can determine the height, weight, age and sex of a person just from a footprint in the sand. We integrate them into special units in the army and they are highly respected for their experience and professionalism."

Ariel turned toward me.

"So, Vered told me you are from Germany. What did you parents do during the war. You are Jewish, aren't you?

I knew that Vered's lie wouldn't last long, but I also realized that I had to protect her.

"Well, my parents came to Germany after the war and my father is not Jewish. I was born, grew up, and live there and study dentistry."

This stretch of the truth seemed to satisfy his curiosity, at least for the present, and the mention of my professional training increased my standing in his eyes. I felt miserable to have lied, and it was clear how uncomfortable I was when talking about my origin and nationality. Shame and denial had crept into my life. For now, I thought, maybe it was easier to be dishonest than to express the truth. But this later proved to be the wrong approach as my identity developed.

Vered finally entered the dining room, but she sat at another table where she chatted with her friends. My displeasure at this must have been obvious, and Ariel laid his hand on my shoulder.

"You have to learn one thing in this young kibbutz. We share everything. I mean everything. Do you get it?" he grinned.

No, I didn't get it, and I had to admit that my feelings for her were beyond infatuation. But I also knew that the next morning I would have to leave her behind and go back home.

To shake off those thoughts, I stood up and left the dining room. Outside I walked toward the street and was greeted by a breathtaking and unobstructed view of a mountain ridge on the Jordanian side of the desert. The setting sun painted the mountains an intense orange and I stood there for minutes fascinated by the view.

Suddenly, I noticed that Vered was standing right beside me.

"Now you know why I love the desert. I could live here forever. Away from the congested and loud city. Away from all the politics and the troubles. Just wide open space. Would you like to stay here?"

"I don't know. Maybe for a while," I answered.

"I really regret that we have so little time with each other. You know I am in the army and have to stay here. I would love to show you more of my country and hope that you find your way okay when you go back tomorrow."

"Yes, don't worry about me. I will be fine," I lied, silently admitting that she was one of the main reasons I had come.

The sun had almost set and it was quickly getting darker and cooler.

"I am tired," she said. "Lets go back to the room."

She took my hand and we silently walked back. After entering the room she hugged me.

"You are a good friend. Israeli guys always take advantage of me."

We stood in the dark for an eternity in a gentle embrace and I knew that we had yet to explore the potential depth of our relationship. She finally touched my face and we looked into each others eyes both filled with tears.

"I don't know if we ever will see each other again," she said, "and I hope that you find the peace you are seeking."

I did not know what to say, and she expected no answer. We lay on her bed caressing each other the entire night, knowing that we would separate in a few hours. Finally we fell asleep until the intense light of the early morning sun woke us up.

"You have to get ready. The bus to Jerusalem will be here soon."

I reluctantly got up and turned towards her. She forced a smile, strands of her golden hair covering part of her face.

"Let me get ready. I will take you to the bus stop."

Silently, we both dressed and left the room, each filled with our own desires and dreams. Ariel was waiting with his pick-up truck, smiling dryly at our gloomy expressions. He took us to the main street, and as I left his truck he called out,

"You are an interesting guy, Bernd. Come back one day and spend longer in this country. I am sure you will stay."

"Maybe one day. Maybe. Thanks for everything and shalom." I did not know yet that his prediction would eventually become true.

Walking towards the bus stop, Vered clutched my hand hard. When the bus arrived we hugged for a last time and I gently caressed her face and softly kissed her lips. Tears were running down her cheeks as she hugged me.

"Shalom. I hope that we will see each other soon."

She nodded silently, but both of us knew that the future was unpredictable. I boarded the bus and sat next to the window. She pressed her hand against the glass, and so did I, until the bus slowly moved forward, separating us. I turned to watch her waving, her blond hair illuminated by the sun, until I lost sight of her.

I did not know yet that it would be the last time I ever saw her.

"Shalom, my desert flower. I will never forget you, "I whispered.

THE FOURTH DAY

ABOARD THE BUS, I felt numb until we reached Jerusalem in the early afternoon.

Without her presence, I had lost my sense of purpose here in Israel. I had to ask myself if I was there for her or for myself. Had my emotion and love for her clouded my determination to seek the truth?

Yes, I had to admit that she had triggered my desire to come to Israel, but I still knew that I had come for more than physical and emotional intimacy. I tried without much success to look ahead, to remember my desire to explore my spirituality.

Arriving in Jerusalem I had two struggles. I struggled to get out of the crowded bus station, and also fought the urge to take the next bus back to the kibbutz. Before I could act on the latter urge, I purchased a few telephone tokens or *asimonims* and called my friend Chalid in the nearby Arab village of Abu Gosh. A man answered the phone, and I managed to gather enough of the Hebrew words I had learned to ask for Chalid.

"Wait a moment," the man replied, and several seconds later I heard Chalid's voice.

"Where are you, my friend? I was hoping for your call."

"I am sorry, Chalid, but I spent a few days with Vered."

I could imagine him rolling his eyes.

"I knew it. She infatuated you and now you are alone and licking your wounds."

"No," I lied. "She just showed me around and now I am here to visit you."

"Never mind. Where are you?"

"At the central bus station in Jerusalem."

"Wait outside and I will pick you up there."

One hour later an old, white, battered pick-up truck pulled up at the side walk and I recognized Chalid in the passenger seat. He jumped out and quickly walked toward me with a wide grin. He embraced and kissed me on both cheeks. I felt awkward, but I had learned that this was the way men expressed their friendship in the Middle East.

"*Salam aleikum,* my friend. Finally you give me the honor of being your host. Come on, let me get your backpack and hop in the car."

I climbed into the crammed back seat of the pick-up finding myself next to another young, slightly overweight man with a broad and friendly face.

"*Keef halak,* How are you?" he asked me.

"My name is Mahmoud. Chalid and I are friends from school and he told me all about you. I want to go to Germany to study engineering and meet those German girls. You know what I mean."

Germany and its people were admired by many Palestinians. I later learned the questionable reasons of their affections for my country, beginning with our skill at soccer.

The driver was a thin but muscular man with gray hear and harsh facial features.

"This is my uncle Mustafa," Chalid said. "He does not speak English and he took us to Jerusalem on his way back from a construction site.

Most of my family work in the construction business. Unfortunately, they cannot work in other Arab countries, such as Kuwait, where they could make a lot of money."

"Why not?" I asked, showing my naiveté again.

"Because we have Israeli passports and are prohibited from traveling to any Arab country except Egypt. I wish we could carry a Jordanian passport like our brothers in the occupied territories. But *Inshallah*, God willing, one day this will change. Let's go home. I want to show you my village, Abu Gosh."

I noticed from his expression and excited speech that he was proud talking about his village.

"Well, Abu Gosh was founded in the 16th century, long before the Jews created the State of Israel. I was taught that the early settlers in the village were Cherkesim, who came from the Caucasus, and Mameluks, who were former slave soldiers who converted to Islam and later formed their tribe. You see, this village has a long history and tradition."

I was intrigued by what he told me. Modern Israel was built by millions of Jews returning from all over the world to the homeland of their ancestors, just as Chalid's ancestors migrated from elsewhere in Eurasia to set claim to the same small piece of land.

"I was thinking, Chalid, that your people have a lot in common with Jews," I said, immediately regretting it. Chalid's head whipped around as though stung by an insect, and his eyes burned fiercely.

"Look, I am a Palestinian. We are all Palestinians who suffer under the Israeli occupation. We were here before the Jews came and now the Jews claim every piece of our land."

Mahmoud, who had been silent until then, jumped into our discussion.

"Bernd, you don't understand. We are Palestinians with an Israeli passport. We are Israelis on paper, but actually we are not treated like we belong here. Chalid and I are among the few young people who attend a Jewish high school in Jerusalem, and we do so only because we want to pass our *Bagrut*, or matriculation exam, and then move on to Hebrew University. But we know we have a slim chance of getting in there or other places in Israel because we are Arabs."

"Why should you have not the same chance as other Israelis?" I asked.

Chalid looked at me.

"Don't be so naïve. That's the way it is. Jews first."

Mahmoud again interrupted him.

"No, it's more complicated. You have to understand that, for example, Israeli men and women go to the army after they finish high school. Then, after two or three years, they come back to begin their studies. So the universities reserve spaces for them, or at least give them preferential treatment."

"But you are an Israeli too. Don't you have to go into the army?"

Chalid and Mahmoud looked at each other, and again Mahmoud answered for them.

"We are Palestinians. We do not go to the army to learn to kill our fellow Muslim brothers and sisters. Druze, Bedouins and Cherkesims serve in the army, but they are not real Muslims. We cannot betray our people."

I tried to phrase my next question carefully.

"Doesn't that mean that you have to accept the consequences of not serving in the army?"

This annoyed Chalid and he answered angrily.

"You have no idea what's going on here in this country. It's your first visit here. You were hanging out with this Jewish girl for to long and now your head is spinning."

He was correct. I had to learn to keep quiet until I knew more. I was just a visitor and observer.

Mustafa obviously sensed that the discussion had touched delicate subjects and addressed Chalid in Arabic. Chalid respected his uncle's authority and changed the subject.

"Soon we will enter he village. You see the signs?"

We were still driving on the Jerusalem-Tel Aviv highway and I saw a sign in Hebrew, English, and Arabic indicating the exit for Abu Gosh. The exit merged with a small, two-lane road that led us into the village. On both sides of the road were several-story buildings constructed in a similar fashion. Thick blocks of Jerusalem stone formed the walls, and almost all had a flat roof with a set of solar panels to provide hot water. Several of the buildings had a second and even a third floor, each in a different style, indicating later construction.

"Why do those buildings look different?" I asked.

"Oh, you mean the additions," Chalid replied, smiling.

"You see, it's difficult to get a building permit even in our village and therefore young married couples just build their home on top of their parents' house."

The car came to a stop in the middle of the village and a group of curious children surrounded the car. Mustafa was yelling at them to step back, but they retreated only a few feet. When I stepped out of the car several young boys and girls touched my hand shouting.

"Almani, Almani!"

"Almani means German," Chalid was saying. "I have told them that you are German, and Germans are very popular among Palestinians."

"Why is that?"

"Well, it has great soccer players, it's a beautiful country, and we heard that German girls like Palestinians. Let me show you my home. It's right up there at the beginning of the slope." He pointed at a two-story building and we walked toward it on a small, unpaved road. A wall surrounded the house and we entered a small courtyard through a metal gate. A middle-aged woman wore a headscarf that framed a face already wrinkled by a life of hard work. But her dark eyes emanated energy and warmth as she shook my hand and spoke rapidly in Arabic.

"This is my mother," Chalid smiled. "She asks me to tell you that this house is your home and as my friend you can consider yourself to be part of this family."

We entered a sparsely furnished living room with several sofas and an oval table in the middle that reached just above my knee. A few fading pictures of a handsome man and woman hung on the wall. Across from the main entrance a large framed poster of the Temple Mount with the Al-Aqsa mosque was visible to all.

His mother was eagerly pointing toward the couch, and I finally understood and sat down. Soon several younger women entered with large plates loaded with fresh grapes, apples, oranges, dates, and other fruits I did not recognize. They also brought small dishes of almonds, nuts, and individually wrapped pieces of chocolate. They were giggling and looked at me curiously, but left the room as soon as they put down their plates.

"These are my sisters," Chalid told me.

"How many siblings do you have?"

"Five brothers and six sisters, and we all live in this house with my grandfather and uncle. We Arabs have large families, because children take care of their parents, and the parents want to guarantee that someone will look after them when they are old or sick. We don't believe much in government. Most families belong to a clan and all of us know and help each other. That's the way it is here in my village."

I didn't notice that I had been handed a plate of fruits and dates, and Chalid was already peeling and cutting an apple for me.

"Here you are our guest. We will take care of you now. Just relax and eat."

I truly enjoyed the sincere hospitality, which I later learned was typical of this village and of Palestinian society at large. Once introduced as a friend of the family, I was embraced as their own.

Again the small army of giggling girls entered the room offering sweet and steaming tea. Soon the room was filled with the pleasant aroma of *nana, or* mint.

"Come, finish your food. Otherwise my mother will think you don't like it," urged Chalid. I tried politely to decline, but my request was ignored and soon my plate was filled again.

A thin middle-aged man entered the room with a cigarette dangling from his mouth. He wore a blue overall suit and a baseball hat covered with drops of dried paint. Prominent cheekbones framed his face and his skin was wrinkled and dry. He appeared drained and tired, but smiled at his son. Chalid immediately stood and kissed him twice on his right and left cheeks.

"*Saleim aleikum,*" said the father after Chalid introduced me. In halting English he apologized for his appearance and asked me to sit down.

Turning towards Chalid he continued speaking in Arabic, asking his son to interpret.

"My father wants to welcome you to his house. He is pleased that you honored his house by visiting us and asks that you consider yourself as part of the family. As builder and developer he greatly admires Germans and Germany because of their achievements in construction and design of cities and modern architecture." Turning towards me he grinned and added,

"Mercedes, Number One."

Again, I was encouraged to eat and the giggling girls reappeared, this time offering a sweat and strong coffee with a nut flavor.

"The coffee tastes peculiar. What is it?" I asked.

"Chalid smiled. Palestinians make coffee with a spice called cardamom. I will ask my mother to prepare a bag to take home to Germany. Let's finish our coffee and I will introduce you to my friends and other members of the family, but first we need to meet my grandfather, Yusuf.

We walked downstairs to a ground-floor apartment. In front of the door sat an old man wearing a traditional Arab garment tied around the waist by a simple belt and a red–and- white checkered headdress called a *keffiyeh,* held in place by a black rope circlet. He looked at me curiously through his dark eyes. In his right hand he held wooden prayer beads, constantly moving them forward with his fingers. Chalid spoke to him briefly in a respectful voice and immediately a wide grin appeared on his wrinkled face. He smiled through his toothless mouth, uttered short sentences in Arabic, and gesticulated with this hands.

"He wants you to come closer, because he can hardly see."

"How old is he?" I asked.

"Well, nobody knows exactly. He was born during the Turkish rule of Palestine and nobody kept birth records at that time. I guess he must be at least eighty-something."

I approached the old man who was now able to touch my face and hold my hand tightly. He started to talk excitedly and Chalid strained to interpret every word.

"He says that he is proud seeing a German and he welcomes you as his guest. He insists that you stay in this house and allow us to host you."

I nodded to express my appreciation.

"He also says that he served in the Turkish army and later in the British army. During the War of Independence of 1948 he lead a group of villagers to defend Abu Gosh against the approaching invading Arab armies and they provided assistance to the Jewish resistance."

I was surprised to hear this story because I had assumed that Palestinians living in Israel were either forced to leave or to surrender to the nascent Israeli Defense Forces.

"Would you ask him why he did that?"

Chalid was reluctant.

"Why do you hesitate?"

"Because I do not understand it either. I would have fought the Zionists. Maybe things would have been different here if he had." Nevertheless, he finally addressed his grandfather. After understanding the question the old man put his left hand on my forearm and looked into my eyes. He pointed the ring finger of his right hand towards the sky and spoke slowly in Arabic.

"What does he say?" I asked

Chalid listened carefully and then translated.

"We are all Abraham's children. There are no differences between Jews and Arabs. We all pray to the same God, but in different tongues. Our village was built on the ruins of a biblical Jewish town and according to their scriptures, the holy stone tablets were kept here for twenty years before being moved by the Jewish king to their temple in Jerusalem. If this ground was worth being the temporary home for their holy stone tablets, then we Palestinians should honor God's will and maintain our village as a home for Jews and Arabs. We always welcome our Jewish neighbors. I am an old man now, but as long as I live, I want to teach my children, grandchildren, and grand-grandchildren respect for our neighbors and the Jews in general. We never served in their army to fight against our Arab brothers, but we were willing to defend our home against anybody who intended to disturb the peace between us and the Jews, and in the end between us and God."

He held the beads before my eyes.

"There are ninety-nine beads to say Allah's name ninety-nine times after each prayer, thirty-three times *subhan'Allah*, thirty-three times *alhamdou'LillAh*, and thirty-three times *Allahou Akbar*. Saying the prayers will strengthen the bond between Muslims and Allah. I respect this bond and I understand the bond and devotion the Jews have for their God. Once we act accordingly there will be peace. *Inshallah*, God willing."

The old man slowly closed his eyes while continuing to move his lips in a silent prayer. He released his grip of my hand and sank back in his chair.

"Let's go," Chalid said. I continued standing in front of the old man whose faith and commitment to peace and understanding deeply moved me. It was obvious that he lived a fulfilled life, witnessing the profound changes that took place in this land. His message resounded clearly in my mind: faith in and respect for God is the basis for peace and understanding and respect for other human beings.

I later verified his story about the stone tablets once kept here. He referred to the biblical town of Kirjat Yearim, the Town of Forests. According to the scriptures, this town was the home of the Ark of the Covenant for twenty years before it was moved by King David to Jerusalem and later placed by Solomon in the Temple.

According to the Jewish scriptures, the Ark contained the two tablets of stone constituting the evidence of God's covenant with the people. Since the destruction of the Temple the whereabouts of the Ark have been unknown. Some allege it was hidden beneath the Temple Mount; others claim it was taken to Ethiopia.

Chalid was impatient.

"Come on, let's go. My grandfather needs to rest."

I noticed the anger and tension in his tone of voice.

"Why are you angry?" I asked him as we walked.

"Old people always talk about moderation and peace. They got used living with the Jews when they could run their own village affairs. But once you leave the village like I do every day, going to a Jewish high school or just traveling to Tel Aviv or Haifa, you are constantly reminded that we are second-class citizens."

"What do you mean by that? I thought Israeli Arabs have the same identity card as other Israelis and carry and Israeli passport."

He laughed bitterly.

"You are so naïve. Of course on paper everything appears the same. But once you scratch the surface you see the ugly picture. The Jews don't trust us.

At school, my Jewish classmates rarely invite me to their home, introduce me to their parents, or let me stay for dinner. Several times I have invited them here and some showed up and they were treated well. When I walk on Rehov Dizengof in Tel Aviv, I always have the feeling people are looking at me. I feel the tension, as if I do not belong. On the other hand, when I travel to Nablus or Ramallah in the occupied territories my Palestinian brothers look at me suspiciously, because I live here in Israel and am considered to be an Israeli. Some call us traitors just because our grandparents or parents chose to stay in their villages after the War of Independence. Sometimes I ask myself who am I and where I should live to be really independent."

I knew that his words were spoken not out of hatred but frustration. He attempted to live here, but he had yet to find his place in this society, if one existed.

"Tell me, my friend, what's happening with you? I noticed how intently you listened to my grandfather's religious talk. I already had the feeling in Germany that you were looking for something else in your life or beyond. And what's new with Vered, the Israeli girl who infatuated you?"

I hesitated to answer, not wanting to admit that he had put his finger in an open wound.

"Well, I spent some time with her, but left her behind in the kibbutz where she has to stay with the army. I really do not know what to say. Yes, I like her. No, that's not correct. I have feelings for her. But I also know I cannot fall in love with her because such a relationship cannot work out. I live and study in Germany. She lives here in Israel and serves in the army with plenty of guys swarming around her. You are right. She turned my head around and I have to deal with it."

Chalid looked at me sympathetically.

"That's OK. I told you the Jewish girls are like that. But tell me about your spiritual plans. Something is on your mind."

I took a deep breath and sighed.

"I do not belong to any organized religion, even though I was baptized Catholic. I am deeply touched by the Jewish faith and I want to explore it further. That's all I can think of right now."

Chalid listened to me intently and then put his hand on my shoulder.

"You know what the irony is? Don't take it personally. But once you become a Jew you can live here, be granted automatic citizenship, and get all the rights and benefits of a new immigrant. I, on the other hand, was born and raised here, but will always be a second-class citizen. I don't accept that. That makes me and many of my friends angry. We have our lives ahead of us and want to move forward in our chosen careers. We may not want to live in this village any more, but in Tel Aviv or Haifa or wherever we choose, but we cannot do that. Please listen to all sides and try to understand the complexities of life in this small country."

While walking we almost forgot where we were going. Suddenly Chalid stopped and pointed toward another house similar to his.

"Here we will meet my friends. Just hold back with your spirituality talk. They may not understand as I try to do. Promise?"

I reluctantly agreed, but I realized that I had to respect my friend and to keep my mind open. We entered the courtyard of his friend's house and again were greeted by the entire family who accepted the visit by the "Almani" as I was known in the village. Word of my arrival had spread very quickly.

I slowly got used to he same tea or coffee ceremony as an expression of generous and unconditional hospitality, which was typical of all Palestinian families I met. Then we joined a group of young men, all in their early twenties, all of whom spoke passable English. Almost all attended Israeli high schools so they were also fluent in Hebrew. Chalid introduced me to Abed, Saiid, and Ramie.

Mahmoud was also present. He struck me as a silent fellow who always smiled but seemed to radiate an underlying sadness. Later Chalid told me that Mahmoud suffered from mood swings and often could not function. Even as a freshman medical student, I was able to diagnose him as either suffering from depression or bipolar disorder. Unfortunately, he never sought specialized medical treatment, and the cultural constraints of his close-knit society and archaic stereotypes about mental illness prevented him from seeking help. Tragically, several years later Mahmoud's body was found hanging from an olive tree near the village. He was hastily buried in a shallow grave and the family was shunned by other villagers as if they suffered from leprosy.

We all sat down to drink coffee and eat the sweet Arab pastry called *baklava*, made of chopped nuts covered with sugar or honey syrup. As we exchanged pleasantries my Palestinian hosts asked about German women, known here for their preference for Arab men. After so many questions about German and Scandinavian women, I finally had to ask why.

"Why do you not seek partners among women of your village?"

"You don't understand Arab culture," Abed replied. "You cannot just date a woman here and have a casual relationship. It happens, but if the family of the girl or woman finds out, they consider it a dishonor for their family. In order to reestablish the honor, the woman has to be killed by a family member."

"You must be joking," I said, disbelieving.

"No, it has happened in the village on several occasions. The Israeli police arrest the father or brother thought to be the perpetrator, but they only acted according to what our tradition tells us to do. If you want to be intimate with a woman, you either have to marry or try your luck outside the village with tourists or Israeli girls. You can also get married, but that is not so easy, because you have to have a lot of money. You pay to arrange the marriage, to get the family of the bride to release her from their house, and to hold the wedding ceremony. If you do not have a job or a wealthy family, you cannot marry. So we are stuck between trying to uphold the traditions that define our identity, and escaping those same traditions prevent us from moving forward."

Ramie suddenly joined the conversation.

"Tell me more about Germany. I really admire what the Germans did, and especially Hitler."

I almost choked on a mouthful of sweet baklava. I slowly chewed it and cleared the sticky sweetness from my mouth with a glass of water as I contemplated my answer.

"What do you mean?" I asked, trying to conceal my anger and

buy some time.

Chalid immediately understood my reaction, but before he could say anything, and without giving Ramie the time to answer, I decided to speak out honestly.

"Horrible sins were committed in the name of Germany and ordered by Germans such as Hitler."

"But he tried to kill the Jews," Ramie protested. "If he had had just a little bit more time, we Palestinians wouldn't be in such a mess."

"You mean, if he would have succeeded killing all Jews in extermination camps such as Auschwitz?"

"Yes, yes," Ramie nodded approvingly.

"Let me tell you one thing. As a German I am ashamed about what was done to Jews."

Testing the boundaries of their hospitality, I continued:

"I am also shocked that Palestinians, whom I considered to be intelligent people, would approve of such terrible actions. I understand your anger and frustration, but consenting to Hitler's policies of murder won't buy you any support in Germany."

My hosts were perplexed by my candor, but I was not done yet.

"By the way, do you know that Hitler and all of his Nazi supporters were anti-Semites?"

Ramie looked at Chalid, Abed, and Saiid and almost simultaneously they answered.

"Yes, of course we know," Chalid said.

"So if you know that, you probably are also aware that the term Semite is derived from Shem, one of three sons of Noah. Shem's descendants are Aramaeans, Assyrians, Babylonians, Chaldeans, Sabaeans, and Hebrews. Therefore you are Semites, too, just like the Jews. Hitler's goal was to root out all Semitic ethnic groups, as well as gypsies and many others classified by the Nazi ideology to belong to 'inferior races' as they called them. He would not have stopped by cleansing the world of Jews. He would have moved on sooner or later to the Palestinians."

Chalid and his friends looked at me wide-eyed. Of course I had oversimplified the facts in order to hit them with the punch line about the Palestinians, but I was so angry that I had to get my point across.

Chalid finally cleared his voice.

"I never knew that," he said, and the others nodded in agreement. "And I apologize for upsetting you."

"Actually, I am glad that I was asked the question, because it provides me with the opportunity to tell you that Germans may sympathize with the Palestinian cause for more rights and statehood, but they reject any violence to reach that goal. We had our share of terrorism in Germany in the last ten years, when the Red Army gangs caused great turmoil, but they were later all killed, arrested or committed suicide. Furthermore the Palestinian terror attack against Israelis at the Munich Olympics disgusted many Germans."

"But because of it, the world is listening to us," Rami protested.

"They may listen to you, but they are hesitant to support you because of the impression that the Palestinians are unpredictable and will resort to violence when things do not work out for them politically."

Rami was not pleased by my description of Palestinian politics.

"I heard that Palestinian causes are supported by a lot of young Germans, who will influence public opinion."

He was right. Palestinians were popular among many young Germans, especially students, who identified with Palestinians' status as refugees and alleged victims of the Israelis. Several left-wing parties and student organizations regularly invited Palestinian activists to speak at their meetings. Those speakers were skillfully trained to depict the Palestinians as the true victims of the Holocaust, which led to the creation of the State of Israel and the expulsion of the Palestinians from their land. Some Germans were eager to shed the feeling of guilt and shame for having committed their own unspeakable atrocities against the Jewish people. They were ready to point the finger at Jews for allegedly perpetrating a "new holocaust" against the Palestinians. My father was one of them, and I later found out that he very much agreed with this thinking because it distanced him from his own personal responsibility.

Chalid noticed that our discussion became adversarial.

"*Chalas*, enough," he admonished his friends. "He is our guest and he must be hungry. Let's eat. Tomorrow I want to show him

Al-Aqsa."

"But he cannot go there!" Saiid protested.

"Why not?" I asked.

"Because you are not a Muslim. Only Muslims can set foot on this holy ground. It's one of the most important of all holy places for us."

Chalid would not be deterred.

"Then we make him a Muslim. I want him to see our holy places. He has seen the Jewish places and he must get to know ours."

I felt uncomfortable during this exchange, just as I had felt when Vered tried to pass me off as a "Jewish cousin."

"I don't have to go," I said. "I want to respect your religious feelings and avoid any offense."

Chalid was determined, but then Saiid said he would not go, and Abed and Ramie nodded in agreement.

"Well then it will be me and Mahmoud," Chalid dryly remarked. "Nevertheless, let's invite our guest to eat."

This suggestion seemed to pass without controversy, and Ramie left the room to ask his mother to bring the food.

Within a few moments plates of steaming rice, vegetables, stuffed grape leaves, lamb, chicken, falafel, and dozens of other delicious but unidentifiable meat and rice dishes were served. We were literally offered a feast, with freshly baked pita which was torn into small pieces and used to sample everything.

"Enjoy the food, and to your good health, *sahtin*," Abed pointed to the food.

"Thank you, *shukran* and sahtin to you my friend."

It was an occasion to set aside our differences and join together in our meal. Afterwards we were served coffee, fruits, and baklava. At that point my fatigue set in and Chalid recognized that it was time to go. Abed, Ramie, Mahmoud, and Saiid embraced and kissed me on cheek twice, which initially I was embarrassed to return, stiffly receiving their warm embrace. Despite our differences, however, the heartfelt hospitality was overwhelming and touched me deeply.

Chalid walked me back to his house, where I would spend the night. It was dark already, yet the village bustled with activity. A steady chilling breeze descended into the valley, carrying the aroma of the pine trees that surrounded the village. Each household appeared to be playing the radio at full volume, flooding the town with Arab music. Some of it had a fast rhythmic beat, some a slow wailing character evoking emotion and sadness. Stray dogs followed us as we walked and children waved from doorways.

"I like your village," I remarked.

"Yes, but sometimes I wish I could get out of here," Chalid grunted. "Don't misunderstand: I love my village and my people, but this is a small world and I am a young man. Look at you. You can travel anywhere in the world. I am stuck here – little money, no future in Israel, an Israeli passport I can't use to travel to Arab countries. I am stuck." His anger and frustration were clear as he went on.

"I want to get out of here. I think of taking one of the scholarships offered by an Arab political party in Israel that allows young Arab men to study abroad. I want to study dentistry and when I am finished maybe I'll come back." He looked around the village and took a deep breath.

"Or maybe not."

We reached his house and he showed me into a room with a bed prepared for me.

"See you in the morning, my friend. *Leila Sa'eeda*, good night,.."

My eyes closed quickly and it did not take me long to drift into a deep sleep. I was still yearning for Vered's embrace and I missed her very much.

"Good Night, Leila Tov my friend"

THE FIFTH DAY

I SLOWLY DRIFTED OUT of my sleep with the voice of a muezzin's call to morning prayers. I opened the curtain and the window offered a view of the entire village, surrounded by pine trees and blossoming bushes crowned by yellow flowers.

In the village center was the monastery, proclaiming the peaceful coexistence between Christian and Muslim Arabs. Almost two thousand years earlier, a church had been built on the site that was become the village of Abu Gosh. The church was destroyed during the Persian invasion of 614 and a monastery was subsequently built on the remains. The monastery was destroyed and rebuilt several more times and was finally restored by Napoleon IV in 1875. That history was so alive and present in and around Jerusalem and never ceases to impress me.

A knock at the door brought my attention back to the present. I opened the door to find a cup of steaming mint tea, a fresh towel, and bar of soap. I quickly made use of them, got dressed, and went downstairs where Chalid and Mahmoud were sitting in the living room.

"Good morning, *sabah alkahir,* my friend. Did you sleep well?"

"*Sabah alnur,*" I tried. "Good morning to you."

He smiled at my effort to learn Arabic phrases.

"Soon you are going to speak Arabic. We will teach you. Now sit down for breakfast."

The meal was simple but tasty and refreshing. It consisted of *labna,* yoghurt cheese, and olive oil and bread. Chalid taught me to dip the bread into the oil and then into wild thyme called *zata'ar* and then into the labna. It was a simple but delicious breakfast which at times I still eat today.

"Let's get ready for our adventure in Jerusalem. Today I will make you a Muslim."

Chalid grinned, but to me it didn't seem like such a good idea.

"Chalid, let's think that over. I do not want to get you into trouble."

"Don't worry," he grinned, "You haven't seen how persuasive I can be."

Mahmoud was smiling at me.

"I heard from Chalid that you like the Jews so much that you want to be one."

"I just want to learn as much as I can so that and later I can consider," I answered evasively. I still did not know what to expect or do. The cacophony of new impressions kept triggering conflicting emotions. I needed time to sort them out!

Mahmoud let go of the topic and Chalid pushed us to get ready.

"We have a lot to do today. Let's not waste any time."

The three of took a bus to the central station in Jerusalem. Chalid pointed out a separate terminal for Arab passengers traveling to and from the occupied territories.

"You see, they separate the Arabs from the Jews. They don't trust us. How can there be peace if we do not learn to trust each other in daily life?"

He sounded angry and bitter, but by now I understood his attitude. I felt that as an outsider I should not take sides, but it was difficult to remain impartial in the face of so many perceived injustices.

A taxi dropped us off at the Jaffa Gate, painfully reminding me of Vered. I missed her company, but I had to keep moving. This time the walk through the Arab quarter of the Old City was a totally different experience. Mahmoud and Chalid chatted with the vendors, joking and smiling. Most invited us to enter their small stores, which from the outside appeared to be nothing more than holes in the wall. Inside, however, those small shops were filled with a dazzling array of goods ranging from cheap items for tourists to beautiful handmade vases, ornaments, silver jewelry, and traditional Arab clothing. In every store we were offered coffee and tea and I started to feel comfortable among the Palestinian Arabs.

Chalid pointed out posters of the Al-Aqsa mosque, which were placed prominently in every store I entered.

"Al Aqsa is the heart of *El Kuds*," he said, calling Jerusalem by its Arabic name. "It's the symbol of our continuous presence, which cannot be wiped out by the Jews. All of us try to pray there, to express our solidarity with El Kuds."

I was tempted to remind him that during the past centuries Muslims always had access to the Al-Aqsa mosque, whereas Jews were forbidden to visit the Western Wall until they seized the upper hand in 1967. Being among Palestinian Arabs in very heart of the Arab Quarter, I did not raise the issue.

"Now it's time to visit the Al-Haram al-Qudsi al-Sharif," Chalid said, using the Arab name for the Temple Mount. We walked through the narrow pathways of the Old City, passing through the Jewish Quarter and the entering the area facing the Western Wall. Just a few days earlier I had prayed in this very spot and met the mysterious old man who looked through a window into my soul. Today I searched for him in vain.

Right next to the Wall a ramp ascended to the Temple Mount, but halfway up a guardhouse prevented direct access. Several policemen inspected every person entering the Temple Mount.

"Chalid, do you really want to go through with your plan?" I asked.

"Sure. Don't worry. I know a policemen who is related to a cousin of mine. Don't worry. It will be OK."

I was not convinced, and as we slowly approached the gate I grew increasingly nervous. I did want to visit the Temple Mount, but I knew that it was forbidden for Jews to visit the Arab Holy Sites. I also knew that in 1969 an Australian fundamentalist Christian had set the Al-Aqsa mosque on fire, and ever since then the Muslim administrative body, the *waqf*, responsible for the Haram-al-Sharif in Jerusalem, had forbidden access by non-Muslims, some called *infidels.* This was made very clear by a large and prominent sign in English, Arabic, and Hebrew, endorsed by the Chief Rabbinate of Israel.

One of the guards was already approaching me and it was too late to turn around. He was a middle-aged man with a large mustache and a serious expression.

"*Shismak?* What's your name?" he asked in Arabic. I didn't know what to say and mumbled the few words I knew in Arabic.

"Ana Almani, I am German."

He grinned and continued in English.

"My brother lives in Germany. He studies engineering in Hannover. But what are you doing here? You should know that I cannot let you in here unless you are a Muslim."

At that moment, Chalid managed to push himself through the waiting group of Muslims.

"*As-salam alaykum,* he is a friend of mine from Germany. I want to show him the Temple Mount to teach him about our culture."

I was relieved that he had obviously given up the idea of introducing me as a Muslim. The guard hesitated, then looked at me.

"I will let you in, but you cannot enter the mosque during prayer.

Do you understand me?" I nodded and before I knew it we were pushed forward by the crowd. Chalid and Mahmoud just smiled at me.

"You see?" said Chalid. "It was that easy. Now you can see why we are so proud of our mosque."

After passing the gate we entered the flat-topped area of the Temple Mount which was large enough to hold tens of thousands of people for prayer. It was surrounded by a continuous wall with multiple gates, one of which is called the Golden Gate. According to Jewish belief, the Messiah would enter Jerusalem through this gate. The Al-Aqsa mosque was located in the southernmost part of the Temple Mount area and consisted of several halls capped by a silver dome. On the opposite side, almost touching the top of the Western Wall, was the Dome of the Rock.

"I suggest visiting the Dome of the Rock," Chalid said, "because you cannot enter the mosque during the Friday prayers." We hurried toward the octagonally-shaped building with its bright gold-foiled dome and exterior cover of porcelain tile. Inside a stunning display of hand painted Byzantine tiles formed a variety of circular and oval decorations, painted windows, and doors, and multiple inscribed Arabic texts from the Koran. It was a dazzling sight.

"And you have to see that," Chalid said, pointing now to a fenced area surrounded by carpets. The area contained a large, flat stone bearing multiple indentations. "This is where our prophet ascended on his horse Buraq to heaven."

"Actually, that is not really correct," Mahmoud said. "From here our prophet Muhammad returned from heaven after ascending from Mecca. During this journey, when he consulted with Moses and was given the Islamic prayers before returning to earth, the angel Gabriel accompanied him. Therefore, this site is one of the holiest places in Islam."

"Isn't it amazing that all three major religions had sprung from this same site, from this very rock," I said.

"What do you mean by that?" Mahmoud asked, as Chalid looked at me curiously.

"Well, according to the Christian scriptures and the Jewish Torah, this stone is the site where Abraham was asked by God to sacrifice his son Isaac; he was going to obey until he was stopped by God. For Muslims, this is the holy site where the Prophet returned to earth after receiving holy prayers from God. There are so many things in common between these religions. Why do they fight each other?"

Chalid looked at me and replied calmly.

"Because Jews don't understand that Islam is the continuation of God's revelation to mankind. First to the Jews through Abraham and Moses, then for Christians through Jesus, and finally through our prophet. Actually, Jews should recognize Islam as the modern version of God's will. If that happens, there will be peace."

"That means that Muslims do not recognize Jews' or Christians' right to their own religion?"

"No, no," Mahmoud interjected. "You misunderstand. We recognize and respect them. Don't forget that the great Saladin, who liberated Jerusalem from the Crusaders in 1187, treated all Christians and Jews remaining in the city as his guests and did not murder and slaughter them, as the Crusaders did of the Muslims eight-eight years earlier when they captured Jerusalem. Islam is a religion of peace. Christians and Jews can always live together with Muslims, but they need to respect our special relationship with the Almighty."

I couldn't resist continuing my line of questioning, because their explanation did not satisfy my curiosity.

"I still do not get it. What you just told me sounds like a self-righteous attitude and an attempt to rationalize a dominant role of Islam. It appears to me that unless everybody converts to Islam they cannot understand God's will. Is that right?"

Mahmoud and Chalid looked cautiously around us.

"Please," asked Chalid, almost pleadingly, "do not raise your voice. These walls have many ears and there are people here that do not see things the way you do." He appeared almost scared.

"Let's leave," I suggested. "This place stirs up too many emotions."

We exited the mosque as the sun was slowly setting in the West, illuminating the dome with an orange glow. From the nearby Al-Aqsa mosque the voices of people at prayer could be heard, and from the Western Wall came the collective murmur of Jewish prayers. They all seemed to merge into a guttural symphony of pleading at the doorstep of the Almighty.

We silently walked toward the gate, down the pathway, and across the large area in front of the wailing wall, which was now bathed in floodlight.

"Let's take a cab to the bus station and from there the bus to the village," said Chalid. "Tomorrow morning you have to get up early to travel to Haifa to catch your ferry back home."

I realized I had not thought about returning home to Germany for almost all of my five days in Israel, five days that seemed like a lifetime. My experiences had been so intense that I knew I had to come back for more.

We reached the village late at night, and Chalid's mother got up to prepare us hot tea and Arab pastries. Soon afterward I went to bed and sank immediately into a deep sleep, overwhelmed by impressions of the last few days.

THE DEPARTURE

IT WAS STILL EARLY when Chalid woke me.

"Sabah ala-kheir, Good morning my friend. You have to get up and get ready. My uncle and I are taking you to Haifa in half an hour." I was surprised by his offer, because even under the best conditions it would take at least three hours to drive one-way to Haifa.

"Don't worry. I don't want you to get lost, and this leaves us some time together."

I hurried to get ready and just had time for a cup of the delicious Arab coffee before we left. I wanted to say good-bye to everybody, but only his mother, sisters, and younger brothers were home. His mother shook my hand and spoke rapidly in Arabic, which Chalid tried to interpret.

"My mother wants to let you know that you and your entire family would be welcome to return here as our guests. You are now part of the family. May Allah be with you and provide peace and prosperity for you."

His mother cried when I left and got into the waiting car. A large group of children chased the car screaming

"Almani, Almani, maa salama; goodbye, German guy, goodbye."

I sank into the back seat, sitting next to Chalid.

"I missed saying good-bye to Mahmoud. Where is he?"

Chalid looked at me sadly.

"You know Mahmoud sometimes has bad days when he just locks himself into his house. I wish I could help him. Since we finished high school together he has had more of those episodes. I guess he doesn't see a future for himself, and that depresses and frustrates him. Don't misunderstand me. This is a great country and I have benefited from its system of education. But still I do not feel that I belong here and neither does Mahmoud."

He looked out the window as we passed through the Israeli villages and small towns with their small, neat houses, orchards brimming with oranges. Beyond them were endless fields of cotton.

"You see the Jews really have changed this country. For the better, I have to admit, but we are left behind to do the menial jobs. When I worked with my father in construction, all the Jews called me Ahmed."

"Why did they call you Ahmed?"

"Because it was the only Arab name they remembered, and they used it for every Arab on the construction site. It made me angry. I grew frustrated seeing my father in that position of servitude, as if he was waiting for crumbs swept off the table. No, I don't think I can live here unless things really change. I want to be a doctor like you, and I decided to study medicine or dentistry in an eastern European country. Maybe I will come back, maybe not."

"Do you get along with your father?" I asked.

"Yes, of course, in our society we respect our parents and help them when they need our help. I know that my father sacrifices his life to help us get high school and university degrees. He can hardly read and write, but he is a dedicated and smart man. I know that his servitude toward the Jews is based on the fact that he needs the jobs they offer him."

Chalid turned towards me with a puzzled look.

"You haven't told me much about your father. Why is that?"

I hesitated, those feelings of shame and guilt surging back and forth in me.

But Chalid was reading my mind.

"I know why you are reluctant to speak about him. It has to do with Germany's past and your father's involvement. Now I understand your fascination with the Jews and your interest in their culture. You feel guilty and want to make good for what your father has done wrong. Don't you? I respect that, but I need to let you know that you are forgetting one thing. If you Germans hadn't committed those horrible crimes, we Palestinians would had have an easier life."

I didn't know how to answer, in part because I understood his thinking, and because my father had unwillingly played an important role in steering my interest toward Judaism, the people and their faith. And though I knew that I was not personally responsible for the events leading to the Holocaust, I still couldn't – and shouldn't – escape our collective responsibility. And yet it had brought about the creation of a Jewish state which Chalid felt was oppressing him and his people.

"You are correct, my friend. It was my father who triggered my interest in Judaism, but I made the personal decision to pursue the issue, and it was not based on guilt."

"As long as you are sure about that, I understand," Chalid replied. "But I hope you have experienced the other side of this society. We are still living in the shadow of the Holocaust, and my people are sympathetic to the suffering of the Jews. Nevertheless, Jews should have learned that their suffering does not justify the suffering of another people."

"Why are you considering yourself a victim of history? It appears to me that Palestinians can make their own decisions and enjoy similar rights as all other Israeli citizens," I replied.

Chalid sighed.

"My friend, that may be partially true, but we are a proud people and our identity should be recognized. It's hard to consider myself an Israeli as long as Israel's nationality is based on Zionism and a religious idealism. So far the term Israeli is synonymous with Jewish faith and history. Once they untie that knot and secularize the Israeli nationality, then I may feel more comfortable and even at ease. Until then, I am living with a split personality: Israeli and Palestinian. I hope you understand. Do you?"

I nodded in agreement, while grudgingly admitting to myself that I only partially understood. I still had a difficult time comprehending his anger and resentments.

Maybe, because I still had problems defining my identity, and when later in life I came to terms with myself, I also was able to understand Chalid's identity conflict.

Meanwhile, we had arrived in Haifa and were approaching the harbor. This time I was not looking forward to boarding the ferry, knowing that I would have to depart from a country I admired and people whom I had learned to love and respect. The car came to a stop at the gate close to the customs building.

"We have to say good-by here," Chalid said. "Don't forget me, don't forget what you have experienced and learned here. The long trip home will provide you with ample time to think about your life. What ever you decide, I will still be your friend." He handed me a big bag filled with bread, cheese and fruit.

"My mother prepared this for you. She knew that you would have a long journey, and it contains all your favorite foods."

I was speechless and tears filled my eyes.

"Lets say good–bye, my friend, ma'a salama." He embraced me and kissed me on the cheeks, and this time I was able to reciprocate.

He turned back to the waiting car and I waved until it was lost from sight. I looked around the gate, foolishly expecting to see Vered, but she was far away. I missed her painfully and longed for that final embrace. Finally, I walked slowly through the gate and boarded the ferry.

This time I made sure to find a covered seat on deck, and caught a final glimpse of Haifa. A city with a magical appeal. A city and country where I would leave my heart.

Shalom Israel, shalom my friends. I will never forget you. I will come back.

CHAPTER 3

METAMORPHOSIS

THE LONG TRIP HOME was a blur. Nobody and nothing around me mattered; I lost all sense of time. I ate only what Chalid's mother had packed for me. I missed Vered terribly and longed to spend more time with her. I was confused by the societal conflicts I had witnessed and, most of all, felt the emergence of a deep spiritual yearning. I spent the long and lonely trip awash in confused reflections on my short life, my family, and my future.

I had never been a religious person, and had received hardly any religious education as a boy. True, my mother sent me to a Catholic kindergarten, but the experience felt more like physical deprivation than spiritual education. My mother also insisted that I receive Holy Communion and serve as an altar boy, but none of those experiences brought me any sense of spiritual meaning or fulfillment.

I went over and over my upbringing, the conditions that had shaped my early life. It was clear to me that I had a strong sense of social justice and could not conform to the social norms accepted by my parents. I remembered watching in awe a demonstration of university students in Bamberg in 1966, the early phases of the student revolt in West Germany.

"They should all be thrown in camps," a bystander next to my father had said. "Under Hitler such a thing would never be tolerated." My father merely clenched his fists and remained silent, either because he strongly disapproved of the behavior of the demonstrators, or to express his displeasure about the remark he had just heard. But he remained silent and chose not to respond. I was too young to comprehend, though old enough to detect his anger, but I did not yet have the courage to ask him direct questions. I do remember my surprise that my father, whom I considered to be a hero, did not speak up. He was noticeably angered, but his silence seemed to condone the remarks. It was the first time my father had disappointed me.

Several years later, during my high school years, I took advantage of the increasing openness of the postwar educational system and enrolled in classes in politics, philosophy, and religion. I idealized societies which I imagined as having an ideal system of governance and rule. I naively admired Communist and Socialist ideologies and consumed glorifying propaganda literature from China, the Soviet Union, and Communist East Germany. I was led to believe that those societies had succeeded in addressing people's needs and creating egalitarian and just societies.

I joined the youth movement of the ruling Social Democratic Party, formed a progressive student group at my school, and published a short-lived political magazine. Soon afterward, I was elected school speaker, which resulted in endless conflict and friction with the administration and almost lead to my expulsion. I recall that my father was able to talk to the principal and calm emotions, and I am sure that my stellar academic performance helped, too.

In those days I considered religion to be the antithesis of social progress and justice. I was convinced that faith and religion existed to anesthetize people to make them forget their miserable lives. Seeking a way to find the truth and reconcile myself with the world, I consumed books by Karl Marx, Erich Fromm, Mao Zedong, and others.

All of these activities distressed and worried my parents, of course. My mother even removed political literature from my room and showed it to my father. One night he entered my room unannounced, agitated and angry.

"Your mother and I are deeply concerned about you and your life," he said.

"You are bringing books into our house that insult our entire life and us. We have experienced the Communists first-hand. Your mother fled her home with a pistol in her hand, a pistol I gave her to defend herself against marauding Soviet soldiers. We knew that they were raping and killing German girls and women. You don't know what the Communists have done to Germany."

His predictable speech annoyed me more than his invasion of my room.

My room was my world, and I decorated the walls with left-wing propaganda posters just to discourage my parents from entering and snooping around.

I immediately snapped back,

"I guess the Communists deserved their chance to go marauding after what the Germans did to their country and people. You killed millions of them and never admitted it."

I immediately felt sorry for saying such a thing, but I was too proud to apologize. He stormed toward me, his face red and the middle finger of his right hand pointed at me.

"You dirty bastard!" he screamed. "I am sorry I have to call you my son."

Even in his rage I could detect a silent cry of pain in his tone.

"I tried to educate you to respect your parents, to respect your country, and to be a law-abiding citizen. What did I get? A Communist and a stain on the family's honor. You should be ashamed of what you just said."

Standing face to face with my father, looking into his red, bloodshot eyes and smelling the steaming mixture of alcohol and anger on his breath, I felt remorseful. But my stubbornness prevented me from uttering the simple sentence: I am sorry.

"Maybe I am like my Uncle Karl," I said. "He at least stood for something and stood up against the Nazis."

My father shuddered when he heard his brother's name.

"I don't want you ever to mention his name in this house. For me, he does not exist any more."

"But he is alive and I have the right to know more about him. At least he may tell me more about you than you will."

Instead of responding to my obvious desire to know more about his brother, my father decided to cut our heated discussion short.

"Nothing good will come of talking with him. His mind was poisoned and he will only confuse you more than you are already. But I cannot stop you from seeking him out."

Weeks of tension and silence followed this encounter. It was several months later, in May 1977, that my father unexpectedly offered me the opportunity to join a group traveling to West Berlin, then still an enclave within Communist East Germany. The trip was organized by the German Ministry of Internal Affairs to provide a political perspective on the situation of the divided Germany. I was unsure about the reasons for my father's generosity, but suspected several motives. First, he was conceding my right to get to know a member of our family I had never met, and secondly, he hoped that through the visit I would see and have to acknowledge the truth of what the Communists had done and stood for.

I eagerly accepted his offer, and used the opportunity to visit East Berlin, which at that time was the capital of the former East Germany, the so-called German Democratic Republic. Regarding the second point, he turned out to be correct. After having been scrutinized by stony-faced border guards and passing the border checkpoint, I entered the eastern part of the city, expecting to see the promised land. Instead, I encountered grim-looking people rushing by, empty shelves in grocery stores, and bookstores devoid of anything remotely critical of any feature of this "workers paradise." As I strolled through the city I noticed that several plainclothes policemen followed me everywhere.

Years later I learned that the State Security Services, also known as *Stasi*, kept track of every visitor and citizen in the country, even using family members to spy on one another.

I also noticed that only the buildings in the vicinity of the border crossing appeared modern and well kept; the rest were dilapidated and gray.

I went into a restaurant in search of a hot meal, finding instead defiance and hostility once I was recognized as a western visitor. One woman eyed me disapprovingly from another table.

I gave her a friendly nod and she immediately stood.

"You Westerners are poisoning our society," she loudly announced. "Get out of here." Her behavior was clearly aimed at the plainclothes policeman in the back of the restaurant who surely approved of her "patriotic" behavior.

I paid for a meal I could not eat and hurried back to the border crossing. Obviously, Communism had either not succeeded in ridding

society of authoritarian thinking or required it in order to survive.
I did not detect any progressive elements in this repressive society
which required a wall to separate its citizens from the West – and from
any influences that might lead them to question its authoritarian and
rigid system.

Ironically, it was a political system modeled on the same totalitarian
principals promoted by Adolf Hitler.

At my hotel I dialed my uncle's phone number. A youthful voice
answered:

"Yes, how can I help you?"

"My name is Bernd. Bernd Wollschlaeger. I am Arthur's son."

A long silence was followed by an even longer sigh.

"And how is my brother? I have heard about him only from your
mother, who sends me letters and postcards."

"I don't know what to say," I answered. "I do not know him very
well."

"So nothing has changed in all these years. Come over and talk.
There is so much to talk about."

I did not hesitate to accept his invitation, and one hour later I
stood in front of a large apartment complex scanning the endless
list of names. There it was, Apartment thirty-five, Karl Wollschlaeger,
my uncle.

I rang the doorbell and was buzzed into a hallway leading me to
a bank of elevators. After a seemingly endless elevator ride I found
myself in front of his apartment and knocked on the door. It was
opened by an elderly man whom I immediately recognized by his
resemblance to my father. His eyes were different, however – bright
and youthful, gleaming with optimism and joy.

"Come in my *Junge*, boy," he said, and embraced me. "Let me look
at you." He held my shoulders and carefully inspected my face. "You
look like your father. A spitting image. Are you also as proud and
stubborn as he is? I hope you will learn from his mistakes. Come in
and sit down."

He led me into his scarcely furnished, but nevertheless cozy living
room and offered me coffee.

"He never told me about his mistakes, and I hoped that you could
help me understand him better," I answered.

Karl looked at me intently.

"Of course he didn't. He is too ashamed to reveal that he was mistaken and that everything he did was for the wrong cause."

"He told me that you were a Communist and imprisoned in Dachau."

Karl raised his eyebrows in surprise.

"He told you that? I thought he wanted to bury and forget that issue." He leaned back in his chair and closed his eyes, perhaps reflecting on those dark days he obviously wanted to forget. Then he sat back up and looked at me.

"Yes, your father and I were very different. Arthur always tried to follow the family's tradition serving as a warrior for the glorious fatherland. I, on the other hand, believed that we were being used as cannon fodder for the wealthy industrialists who needed wars to enrich themselves. I refused to serve in the newly formed German army. I joined the Social Democrats and later the Communist party to stand up for a different Germany. Unfortunately, the demagogues and nationalists won, and this maniac Hitler came to power. Your father was blinded by the Nazi ideology and marched to their tune. I tried hard to fight back, but we lost. Many of my comrades disappeared in concentration camps, and after being on the run for years, the Gestapo caught up with me, too. I was in a prison for over a year. I was tortured but never talked. Later I was transferred to Dachau to die. You can imagine my surprise when your father showed up to bail me out. Arthur the war hero, me the condemned traitor. Of course after that your father quickly distanced himself from me, and I spent the rest of the war in a special army unit of condemned soldiers charged with cleaning up minefields. Many of us were torn to pieces by exploding mines but I survived. Maybe your father thought that my death on the battlefield would be more honorable than my demise in a concentration camp. Well, as you see, I survived, and so did your father. After the war I looked forward to rebuilding Germany according to my ideals of justice, but during the Cold War the old Socialists like me were judged to be suspicious elements and I was not permitted to work at certain jobs. I knew that your father, a highly decorated officer, was imprisoned by the Americans for over a year and, once released, confined to a very limited career. The only thing he ever learned was how to be a good soldier and a good officer. He believed in honor and fatherland, and all that was gone. The people he believed in had either fled to South America, died, or committed suicide. Hitler's suicide upset him the most because he could not believe that his Fuehrer would abandon Germany and chose this convenient escape from responsibility. Your father had nothing left but his empty sense of honor, but you can't live on honor, or feed a family with it. So he worked at odd jobs, and that turned him into a bitter man. We were both defeated, each in our own way. Germany was defeated. Germany was totally destroyed, and most Germans lived in a daze of hopelessness. I chose to migrate to East Germany to build a true socialist society, but very soon learned that the Russians believed in the literal interpretation of the dictatorship of the proletariat. They established totalitarian rule and people like me either had to swear allegiance to the Soviet-style Communist party or risk imprisonment. I chose to return to West Germany just before the Iron Curtain came crashing down across Europe. I learned that the era of idealism and ideology was over and just accepted that. Your father was unable or unwilling to learn that lesson, and so we were unable to connect again as brothers."

Visibly exhausted he sank back into his chair and closed his eyes. I was deeply moved as I realized that I was one of the few persons he would tell his story to, trusting that I might learn something from it.

"Bernd," he said, opening his eyes, "tell me what drove you to visit me here in Berlin? I know that your father sent you to me, but what are you looking for?"

I was startled by his directness, but not surprised by his interest in my life.

"I am seeking the truth about my father, my family, my country's past. I cannot accept the idea that silence is the only way to deal with the past."

"You are referring to the Nazi regime and all the horror it inflicted on Germany?"

"Yes, I want to know everything about it."

He regarded me with a mixture of curiosity and sadness.

"I can describe to you in a few words what happened. Too many people looked the other way. Yes, there were upright Germans who tried to resist, but many had to flee, or were thrown into concentration camps. Did you ever hear of Dietrich Bonhoeffer?"

"Not really," I had to admit.

"Well, let me tell you. He was a Lutheran pastor who resisted the Nazis. He was imprisoned and then executed in prison just a few days before the end of the war. He once wrote a famous letter summarizing the prevailing attitude in Germany: First they came for the Jews, and I didn't speak out, because I was not a Jew. Then they came for the Communists, and I did not speak out, because I was not a Communist. Then they came for the trade unionists, and I did not speak out, because I was not a trade unionist. Then they came for me and there was no one left to speak for me."

I listened intently to every word. My uncle seemed to represent the antithesis of my father's character.

"Tell me," I asked, "why is my father so different than you?"

He grinned.

"Because like him, I listened to my father, but unlike him, I stopped believing what my father tried to teach me: trust, honor and love for the fatherland. All of those are fine values when they are applied to your own life. But a ruthless leader can manipulate these so-called values, and use them to abuse the people and the country, and that is what happened to Germany. Your father believed in those false ideas, and our country paid the ultimate price. He attended the NAPOLA, the special training school or "breeding factory" for potential Nazi leaders, and then chose the straight military career. He was a one-hundred-percent believer, even though he never joined the party. He thought about himself as part of an uncorruptible elite of officers. They were above politics, above all mundane affairs, above the real world. But he was used and abused by the politicians. He fought a war he thought was based on honor and respect, and when he was faced with cruelty and barbaric behavior, he looked the other way. I am sure that he knew about the mass killings in the East, but he chose to keep silent."

He put one hand on my right shoulder and with the other he held my chin.

"You are a curious and smart young man. Live your life according to the following principles: tolerance, compromise, and reason. Don't let yourself be mislead by any ideology; distrust even church and faith. Just live your life. It's too short to be wasted or turned over to someone else." He then led me to the door, hugged me, and said goodbye.

I never saw my uncle again, but his words were engraved on my mind.

I turned them over and over in my mind during the long journey home from Israel.

Was I really so different from my father after all? I had to admit that that I, too, was impressed by ideologies and belief systems that promised to establish a rule of men above the rule of God.

I had to remind myself how surely ideologies led mankind into disasters: Stalin's campaign of forced relocation, starvation, and mass killing of millions of Russians, Ukrainians, and other nationalities; Mao Zedong's fanatical "Cultural Revolution" that resulted in the death of millions of innocent victims; Pol Pot's campaign to catapult his country backward into an agrarian Communist state, leaving so many millions dead in the killing fields. My uncle was right that blind adherence to any ideology begins by depriving individuals of rights and eventually brings them suffering, pain, and death.

More importantly, it finally dawned on me that once we remove God from the position of ultimate arbiter of justice, righteousness, and responsibility, we not only minimize their importance but also interpret them according to our own whims. When humans are the arbiters, random murder can be seen as the necessary by-product of progress and revolution; genocide can be justified to protect a self-declared superior race.

I knew that Judaism offered answers to many of the questions that battered my conscience, and I needed to explore it further. But I also had to beware of idealizing any belief system – even my beloved Judaism – or uncritically embracing its promise of a better world under the direction of a Higher Power.

It took me several years to understand that Judaism did not expect blind devotion. On the contrary, Judaism calls upon Jews to demonstrate through ethical and moral behavior that they understand God's commands and can transform abstract commandments into compassionate personal action.

Until now I was neither a religious nor spiritual person. Driven by the arrogance and hubris of my youth, I had discarded religious beliefs as metaphysical aberrations and ridiculed believers as deluded idol worshippers. Growing up in a town in Bavaria inhabited predominantly by conservative Catholics, I had seen how religious rituals, such as the annual remembrance of Christ's crucifixion, could evolve into emotional outbursts of lamentation and mourning that ended up blaming the Jews for his death. So why was I now attracted to another of the world's major religions, and why Judaism in particular? Was it the absence of priests as mediators between me and God? Was it the personal connection with a Higher Power I had felt at the Western Wall? Or was it, as so many people were to suggest, my guilt and shame as a German?

These were the kinds of thoughts and reflections that filled my mind on that long, long ferry ride from Israel to Ancona, Italy. Still in a sober and thoughtful mood, I made my way to the train for the last leg of my return journey, reaching my home town in the late afternoon of a gray autumn day. I did not know what to expect at home when I rang the doorbell. I was greeted by my mother, who opened the door and immediately embraced me tightly.

"I am so happy to see you again. You lost weight. Did you do everything you wanted to do? Did you see Jerusalem?"

She did not stop asking questions, hugging and kissing me.

"Come. It's time to see your father."

I was not looking forward to this encounter. When I entered his study he was sitting in his leather chair reading his newspaper. He looked tired and the almost empty bottle of wine indicated that he had started his drinking early. To reduce the potential for argument, I decided to give only a brief description of my travel and try to avoid provocative topics.

He threw me a brief look.

"You lost weight," he commented dryly. I expected his style of direct questioning, but he said no more, obviously deciding to let me open the conversation.

I was struggling with my desire to reveal to him the life-changing importance of my journey to Israel. He would not understand it, but

I still harbored the hope that he would.

Finally I decided to tell him how I felt about my trip to Israel.

"I found what I was looking for."

"And what did you find?"

"Answers to questions that I had and the truth about many things that I suspected to be true."

The color of the skin on his head turned purple and he roared at me.

"The truth! What do you know about the truth?"

I had certainly failed to avoid provocative topics. Taking a deep breath, I tried another tack.

"More than you want me to. For example, I learned that in spite of perceived pain and suffering, people can forgive. I learned that Jews are people dealing with conflicts within their society and, of course, conflicts with the neighboring Arab countries. I learned that as a German, a representative of a nation that has inflicted so much pain and suffering on the Jewish people, I can turn guilt and shame into ploughshares and help to grow and harvest hope and peace."

My father stared at me with an unfocused gaze. He turned to the very same mantra I had heard so often.

"Why do you have to feel ashamed? I did nothing wrong. We Germans did not know anything about what happened to the Jews until after the war. But that's war. People die in wars. Many Germans died. Have you forgotten that?"

Nothing seemed to have changed for him, while everything had changed for me.

"Father, on that issue, we will always differ. Unless we learn to accept responsibility, we will never overcome denial. What happened to the Jews was unprecedented in human history. Planned mass murder executed in an industrial fashion using death factories with a defined quota of minimum killings per day. I saw the end product. Piles of unclaimed glasses, removed dentures, gold teeth, pictures, and all the other evidence. It REALLY happened."

"It never happened!" my father screamed, slamming his fist on his table. "It's all propaganda. The Jews fabricated this propaganda and you fell for it."

The noise drew my mother into the room. She appeared distraught, surely knowing that my father would behave this way.

"Please stop," she pleaded with him. "Bernd just came home. Let him eat and sleep and tomorrow we can talk."

"There is nothing to talk about anymore," my father grumbled. "His mind is poisoned. He cannot think straight."

My mother pushed me out of the room into the hall.

"Please do not excite your father," she pleaded with me. "You know that since his head injury in the war he has these spells of anger."

I felt like slamming my own fist down.

"Mother, why do you always try to defend him? This story about the head injury is just a pretext you both use to avoid any real discussion. It's time to face the truth and talk about it. I cannot understand why you both try to hide the past from me."

"How can you talk like that to your father and mother?" she cried. "Don't you have any respect?"

At that moment my father stepped out of his room.

"Now you have also succeeded in upsetting your mother. What's wrong with you?"

I stared in disbelief at both of my parents. Having just arrived from the most important journey of my life, I was eager to share my experiences with them, but felt as though we could not even speak the same language. Recognizing that any further effort on my part would only inflame my father's anger, I returned to my room and closed the door. I slumped onto my bed, exhausted and tired from the trip, and fell asleep dreaming about Vered, Israel, and the friends who would at least listen to me, even when they disagreed.

THE DECISION

THE DAYS AND WEEKS after my return passed slowly as I forced myself to return to my dull studies. My academic and practical performance in the field of dentistry left much to be desired, and after having spent a month working as an assistant nurse at a local hospital, I decided to switch to study medicine. I applied for a transfer to another university in the south of Germany, closer to my place of birth. I was always attracted to the jovial and positive Bavarian attitude toward life and the endless outdoor activities available in that region.

My request was granted and I prepared to move to the University of Erlangen, not far from Nuremberg, the infamous capital of Nazi glory and perfidy.

To my mother's great distress, I was moving out of my parents' home for the first time. It was hard for her to let go of me because I represented her hopes and dreams, and maybe because I was the one male figure in her life with a positive attitude.

Just a few weeks before my move, my mother handed me a blue envelope with colorful stamps bearing images of Jerusalem.

"I was hiding the letter from your father. If he had found it, he would have read and destroyed it."

Recognizing Vered's handwriting I waited until my mother left the room and opened it with trembling hands. My face flushed when I started reading and the following sentences forced me to sit down:

"My dear Friend: It has been several months since you left Israel and I hope that you are doing well. I remember the short time we spent together and missed you so much after you left. My mother sends you her warmest regards and looks forward to seeing you again. I am still in the army and met a nice man called Shai. He reminds me of you and we are meant to be together...."

There I had to stop reading as I was blinded by anger and resentment. I had known that our short and intense relationship would not last, but had harbored fleeting hopes that we might at least get back together. Now I knew that I had lost her for good, and tears ran down my face. I should have listened to my friend Chalid, but now it was too late. As my anger slowly abated, I realized that it was better to know the whole truth now than later. Vered had the courage to write to me, and I owed it to our friendship to continue reading.

"...the memory of our short time together will be always engraved in my mind and I hope and pray that you may find happiness too in your life. I know you will. I will always admire the strength of your convictions and feel honored that you shared your thoughts and emotions with me. I have the feeling that one day we will meet again in Israel. Maybe, once you find the truth within you. Love. Your friend forever, Vered."

Since my return from Israel, my daily activities and busy schedule had distracted me from thinking about the issues that had touched me so deeply during my journey. Faith, love, emotion, religion, spirituality – all had taken on meaning for me and revealed a part of me I had never imagined: a soul. I thought I would be afraid to open the gates to my hidden inner self and was reluctant to reveal its vulnerability. But I also knew that my fears were probably based on insecurity and immaturity. Vered's letter had brought these issues back to the surface once again.

Even though her letter made me want to return as quickly as I could to Israel, my next and deeper response was to yearn for my inner self, the true motivating factors and meaning of my life. I decided that I must seek these things, even though I had no idea where to look or what I would find. I had never even practiced the Catholic religion I was born into, and to join another religion in the city of my birth would make me an outcast. I decided that before I enrolled in my new alma mater I would return to Bamberg to revisit the places of my childhood and consider my next steps. Arriving by train from Bonn, I walked all the way from the train station to the old gray building that housed the small local Jewish community. It stood there still, as if frozen in time. The same old garage where I often sought solitude, the same colorless window shutters dangling on corroded metal hooks. The childhood memories were so strong I thought I could hear my mother's voice calling me for dinner and see my father's car pulling up to the curb.

I continued walking, passing the kindergarten and elementary school I attended and then crossing a bridge over the canal to the church where I had been baptized. I entered the church and found the baptism basin. There I visualized the photo taken at my baptism that I later found in a pile of old pictures given to me by my then ill and dying sister. In one picture she held me over a large basin while a priest poured water on my head. While I had no recollection of the ceremony, the picture captured a moment of peace and serenity that I had long lost. This was the same church where I celebrated Holy Communion, a ceremony in which I was deemed mature enough at eight years of age to receive the sacraments as a full member of the Roman Catholic Church. I now felt far from this church and its teachings. As I stood there I was struck by the contrast between my empty Catholicism and the single most serene moment of my life

– when I stood at the Western Wall, immersed in meditation and prayer, feeling my spiritual void fill with a warmth of belonging and connection. I heard again the voice of the mysterious rabbi:

"A lonely neschama seeking a home may have found you and you are carrying this neschama without your knowing." Yes, I was ready to be the home for this neschama and ready to prepare myself for the necessary spiritual transition.

I knew that before I could take the next step, however, I had to close the Catholic chapter of my life. I decided to seek out a priest and confess my intent. I opened the door of a confessional and found myself in a small compartment that forced me to kneel to avoid hitting my head on the wooden ceiling. Soon afterward a sliding screen opened.

"In the name of the Father, the son. and the Holy Ghost," a priest said softly. "My son, have you sinned and are you ready to repent your sins?"

"Father, I am not here to share my sins. I am here to declare my intent to leave the church. I was baptized here and I received my Holy Communion in this church. But I have found my spiritual home in another faith."

After several seconds of silence the priest answered.

"What faith have you found my son?"

"Well, I reached the conclusion that I want to follow God's commands to make this world a better place to live for all of us."

"But the our scriptures have laid out just such a path to follow. Why do you need another faith to achieve this goal?"

"Because I have experienced spirituality as I have never experienced it before. I have prayed like I never have prayed before. I have found that I have a soul and that I am slowly connecting to it."

"My son, you have not answered my question about what faith you want to join."

I hesitated, still not confident about my decision.

"Father, I want to become a Jew."

The priest was silent for several seconds that felt like an eternity.

"Why do you seek faith in a religion that was superseded by our Lord Jesus Christ?"

"I personally do not see it that way. All religions have the right to exist side by side. Nobody holds the keys to eternity. We are all the same with different expressions of our commitment to fulfill the Creator's will."

This answer obviously irritated him.

"My son, our Lord Jesus Christ himself was a Jew and he recognized that he had to move above his own faith to follow God's command and to lead people toward the concept of Christianity."

"Father, again I respectfully disagree. The scriptures described by Catholics as the Old Testament contain rights and duties for us human beings to bring justice to earth and not to defer such justice for a Kingdom in heaven to come. I believe that I can be a partner in this work of redemption and am prepared to take the challenge given by God for his chosen people, the Jews."

"Son, you are committing a grave mistake. You are jeopardizing your soul...."

"No," I cut him off," I do not jeopardize my soul. I have found it, and it's telling me to do something with my life that I am ready for."

Then and there I verbalized for the first time my yearning for spirituality and my struggle to reconnect with my soul. I remembered the words of the mysterious Rabbi in Jerusalem, insinuating that may be I was driven to find what was hidden inside me, recovering my spiritual being and reconciling within myself.

I felt reassured and my resolve strengthened, I had to move forward and now was the time to do it.

As I was leaving the confessional, the priest emerged, too. His rotund face was framed by a remarkably large set of glasses with thick lenses that enlarged his soft, brown eyes. He put his hand on my shoulder and gently tugged my upper body forward toward him.

"I cannot stop you my son, but I ask you to think this over. So much is at stake. Your life, your future, your family. Why do you want to burden yourself with so much responsibility?"

I respected his attempt to convince me to reconsider.

"Father, I promise that what I am going to pursue will be honest and truthful."

He put his hand on my head and blessed me. Without looking back I left the church. Outside I took a deep breath and considered my next move. I knew what I wanted to do, but was also aware that it would put me onto an uncharted path. I crossed the busy weekly farmers' market, but barely noticed the aroma of freshly cut flowers or ripe fruits. I entered the adjacent municipality building, where I searched for the citizen's registry. Once I had found the right teller window, I asked the clerk for a form to formally end my membership in the Catholic church. I completed the form and handed it back to the clerk, who studied it with a disapproving look. I paid a processing fee and received a certified copy of my withdrawal from the church.

"*Dankeschoen*, thank you," I said, but he did not reply. Leaving the building I felt unsure about what to do next, but I was convinced that I had at least done two necessary things.

Later that day, I settled into my new home, the student dormitories at the University of Erlangen. I was assigned a small room with just enough space for a bed and a table. I did not mind the physical restrictions because I had come to focus on my studies and to finally complete my academic degree in medicine.

I also began searching for a Jewish community to connect with, but the phone calls I made to the few small Jewish community centers were met either with suspicion or coolness.

Then I remembered my first encounter with the "Star" as a young boy. I returned to Bamberg, walked to the building that housed the Jewish community, and entered the same hallway I had entered with my mother. There again I faced the star, which I now knew as Magen David and which still magically attracted me.

A large wooden door, decorated with a colorful artwork of glass inlays, formed the entrance. I rang the doorbell and waited. After a pause I heard steps moving toward the door, and then several keys inserted one-by-one to open an array of locks. Finally the door opened and an elderly man of medium height greeted me.

"How can I help you young man. If you look for the dentist, he is upstairs." He was wearing a dark suit with black and worn elbow pads. His face was wrinkled and his grey eyes were sunken in their sockets.

"No, not the dentist, I was looking for someone to talk to."

"Talk about what?" he replied in a raspy voice with a hint of suspicion. He had an eastern European accent I already knew from Israel, indicating that he had probably spoken Yiddish in his youth.

"I, I was in Israel and my father's history and I ..."

He looked into my eyes seeking in them the reason that brought me here.

"You seem like an interesting and nice young man. Maybe I should let you in. What is your name?"

"My name is Bernd," I replied nervously. "I was here in this building before as a young boy and ..."

"We can talk about that later, Bernd. My name is Yaacov Eisenberg. I am the chairman of this community."

I entered a small entrance hall with doors leading into different rooms. Hebrew markings and pictures of synagogues were posted on the wall.

"Come, Bernd. Step into my office." He slowly moved around an old oak table, which reminded me of my father's study. He took off his jacket and sat in a simple wooden chair.

"Quite often people come to visit me here and I feel like a tour guide in a museum.

This is a small community. We have less than thirty members. Most are old – survivors like me."

At that moment I noticed the tattooed number on his right forearm and my gaze froze. He noticed my reaction.

"Don't worry. I have survived and this is my reminder that I made it. I could have had it removed a long time ago, but I chose not too. I lost my entire family in the camps and after the war I found myself a living skeleton in a Displaced Persons camp in Germany. The Americans gave me back my life. I lived in the camp for a while and then moved to Bamberg because the American Army was looking for reliable partners to work with. They gave me an apartment and a job, and I started living again. I ignored the Germans who were at that time trying to get their own lives together, but believe it or not I found a lot in common with those people who killed my entire family. I had the impression that the Germans were as confused and lost as I was."

He smiled at me dryly.

"Isn't that ironic – to live among the murderers of your people. But life has to go on, and I felt too weak and had no more *koach*, strength, to go to Israel to fight or move to the United States to learn a new language. So I stayed here. I met a nice woman, a lovely and warm-hearted *schickse*, a non-Jewish German woman, and we married. She really loves and takes care of me and so here I am, still living in Bamberg."

He knew that talking about himself would relax me, and he was right. Now he reclined in the chair and turned his attention on me.

"So, tell me again why you are here and what you want?"

I told him everything about myself, my father, my life, and my desire to learn more about Judaism. He listened intently and scribbled a few notes on a yellow notepad.

"This is a remarkable story, young man," he said when I had finished. "I have heard many stories, but yours is unusual. What do you want from me?"

"I need some guidance. I need someone who can help me open doors, meet other Jews, and learn. I've found it's very difficult in Germany to meet Jews. They seem to keep a distance from me, a German."

"Can you blame them? After all that happened, they are suspicious and reluctant. You are young and they don't hold you responsible, but there are still Germans living among us who actively participated in the Holocaust and have blood on their hands. It may have dried, but it's blood nonetheless."

I swallowed hard.

"Yes, I understand. Nevertheless, do you think you can help me to learn and study Judaism?"

He looked into my eyes and answered slowly, pronouncing every word.

"You know that according to the Jewish faith I cannot encourage you to convert, if that is what you are seeking. Furthermore, I must warn you that any such decision will jeopardize your relationship with your family, friends, and maybe your career. Especially your relationship to your father, which seems already strained to the breaking point. And if you decide to become Jewish, you most likely cannot find a Jewish woman here in Germany. And if you should find one and decide to have children, how do you want to raise them here? It takes a strong character, a lot of dedication, patience, and faith. I also caution you: Judaism cannot be studied and learned like an academic science. You may be able to do so for the religion, but it's more than a religion. It's a culture, a way of living and even a nationality, if you choose to live in Israel. Have you thought about all that? Probably not."

He was right. I had yet to explore the ramifications of converting to Judaism. I suspected that it would be a challenging and long process, but yet had to comprehend the extent of such a decision.

Yaacov saw my confusion.

"Come, I'll show you around. Too much talk, too little experience." He gently pushed me out of his office and back into the entrance hall. "That's the way to the synagogue. Actually, we have only a little room we use for the rare occasion we can get a *minyan* together."

"What's a minyan?" I asked.

"Oh, let's use that as your first *schiur*, or lesson in real Judaism. To conduct a service in the *Beit HaKnesset*, or house of gathering, also called the synagogue, we need at least ten adult men. That's a minyan. Otherwise we can't start the service and have to pray by ourselves."

We entered a large living room furnished with simple wooden folding chairs. At one end was an elevated platform and on it was a slightly tilted wooden podium covered with a silk blanket. Behind that, a wooden Ark was recessed into the wall and lit by a light suspended from above.

Yaacov took my arm and gently pushed me onto the platform. I was reluctant to go, because I did not want to impose myself and violate any religious feelings.

"Let's continue our lesson. You are standing at the *bima*, where the *tora* scrolls are placed and read, according to the weekly portion, or *parasha*. During the *Shabbat* service on Saturday morning, five to seven men are called upon to make *aliyah*, meaning to go up to the bima, and after reading a prayer, a designated reader chants a section of Torah called parasha. The Torah scrolls are stored here in the *Aron HaKodesh*, or Holy Ark, and are covered with ornaments and a silk cloth. We have about ten scrolls, some of them rescued from the Nazis and hidden in various places during the war. Above the Ark you see a light, which is called the *ner tamid,* or eternal light. Do you follow me?"

I nodded, finding the names and formal order of service confusing.

"One thing you have to understand. Everybody takes part in the religious services. They are communal services that bring us together. We do not need a priest or pope to pray. We can do it by ourselves every day, anywhere and anyhow." Laying his arm around my shoulders he walked me to the door.

"Young man, you have chosen a challenging path. I may direct but not help you. We are a small community and get together only on holidays. There are a few other larger communities in Bavaria and I will contact the chairs of those communities to introduce you. Furthermore, I will also give you the name of a rabbi who may be able to guide you further." He handed me the information and invited me to visit at any time.

That was my first contact with the Jewish community in Germany which then numbered no more then thirty thousand members in its entirety. Before Hitler's rise to power, over six hundred thousand Jews called Germany their homeland.

At first I hesitated to contact the rabbi recommended by Yaacov Eisenberg, but then decided to send him a letter outlining my background, experience, and intent to explore Judaism. I avoided the word conversion, because I knew that I had to grant myself time and have patience. I did not know that many years of learning and waiting lay ahead.

THE RABBI

SEVERAL WEEKS LATER, I received a brief letter in reply from Rabbi Lieberman indicating his interest in meeting me in Frankfurt. He suggested a time and place, and I made arrangements to adjust my studies and free enough time for this meeting. Arriving in Frankfurt on a cold but sunny December morning, I took a cab that dropped me off at a nondescript restaurant in an old downtown building near the Main River.

Entering the restaurant, I noticed a distinctive man in his sixties, dressed in a dark suit, white shirt, and black tie. A large black hat covered his head and he seemed to be deeply immersed in a book.

I approached the table, located in the corner of the restaurant. Only a few other guests were seated, some looking at me curiously.

"Mr., I mean Rabbi Liebermann?"

He slowly closed the book and I could see it was written in Hebrew. As he looked at me I was struck by his dark but bright eyes, which seemed to penetrate my mind. His slightly elongated face was covered with a few wrinkles that almost seemed to have been drawn with a pen along his eyes and mouth.

"So you are the young man who left a lasting impression on my friend Yaacov. He wrote me a long letter all about you. I understand that you want to discuss serious matters with me? Is that correct?"

Still waiting to be asked to be seated, I extended my hand and tried to introduce myself formally.

"No need for that. Just sit down and let's order something to eat first. A man can't talk without having good food and a fine wine." He signaled the waiter.

"Do you like eastern European food? That's what they serve here. I'll make it easy for you and order some soup and the main dish. It's all kosher, one of the few restaurants I visit on my travels through Germany."

I nodded in agreement and finally sat down. I had learned a little about the *kashrut,* or Jewish dietary laws regulating how to prepare food, how to slaughter animals, and what is permissible to eat. Most importantly, those laws determine what is fit for human consumption. At that moment, I remembered only that meat and milk, or anything made with dairy and meat products, cannot be served at the same meal, or cooked as served using the same dishes or utensils, or stored in a way that could cause them to be mixed. But I had no worries about that here, apparently. The waiter handed us the menu, but I was either too anxious or not interested enough to study its contents. The Rabbi noticed my predicament and ordered for both of us.

"You are in for a treat young man. Have you ever eaten *cholent?*"

Without waiting for my answer, he continued. "Cholent is a kind of a stew simmered inside an oven consisting mostly of vegetables: potatoes, barley, beans, carrots, garlic cloves, mushrooms, fried onions. My mother, may her soul rest in peace, always served it as the main course of the Shabbat lunch meal. Eating it reminds me of those wonderful times with her."

I was afraid to ask what had happened to his mother, but he supplied the answer himself.

"My parents perished in Auschwitz and I was sent to England as a child. I returned to Germany many years later to help rebuild the dwindling remnants of the Jewish community."

He sighed and for a moment fell silent as if deep in prayer. After a moment he leaned forward in his chair and spoke to me with some urgency.

"I have read all of what you sent me and I am impressed by your personal history. *Tacheles*, let's get down to business. What is your intent?"

His direct approach surprised me and I tried to organize my thoughts quickly.

"Rabbi, I set out to search for answers to many questions, traveled to Israel, and recognized a spiritual void yearning to be filled. In Jerusalem I had an encounter with a religious man at the Western Wall which left a deep impression on me. There, for the first time in my life, I prayed from my heart and found a soul in me. I still can't describe it, but I know that emotionally I am closer to Judaism than to the faith I inherited at birth."

His eyes half-closed, he listened intently to every word.

"Young man, are you searching for salvation? Is your desire to explore Judaism motivated by guilt about your father's action or inaction?"

"No, or maybe not. Honestly, I can tell you only that I feel personally responsible for all of those horrible crimes inflicted upon the Jewish people by Germans, including my father. But I do not feel guilty. Yes, I am ashamed and the visit to Yad Vashem tore at my heart, but I also learned that we as people have to move forward. Not to forget, but to honor the memory of those perished and to make sure that such a horrendous act will never happen again."

At that moment the waiter appeared at our table holding two plates filled with steaming cholent.

After he left, the Rabbi stood and walked to a small copper-plated sink placed on a small table at the end of the restaurant. Silently saying a prayer, he washed his hands several times using a plastic cup filled with water.

Back at the table, he asked,

"You are familiar with the *netilat yadayim?*"

"Yes, I am," I answered.

"What does it represent?"

"Washing our hands expresses our respect for the body as the sanctuary of the soul. In the *Gemara* they also refer to the washing as a procedure to wash off the bad morning spirits, or *mazikin*.

He looked at me for several seconds.

"I see that you have learned already quite a bit. Have you studied Gemara?"

"No, studying the Gemara and Mishna, the Talmud, was too much for me to tackle then. I just read bits and pieces."

"The Talmud, my young friend, is a record of rabbinic discussions pertaining to Jewish law, ethics, customs, and history, and it takes a lifetime to study it. You have plenty of that ahead of you, if you intend to be a Talmudic scholar."

Turning to the food, he picked up a small loaf of bread from the breadbasket, broke it into two pieces, and spoke a prayer loudly and proudly:

"*Barukh ata Adonai Eloheinu melekh haolam, hamotzi lehem min haaretz.* Blessed are you, oh Lord, our God, King of the universe, who brings forth bread from the earth." He then handed me a piece. "*Beteavon*, enjoy your meal. We need to eat before we talk."

The food was indeed delicious, reminding me of the food I enjoyed eating in Israel. He smiled at my delight.

"You know, this tastes like my mother's cholent. This occasion calls for a drink." He raised his glass of wine.

"*LeChaim*, to life, my friend."

He then gently put his hand on mine and softly asked,

"What do you want to do? Becoming a Jew is a great responsibility and will set you apart in this country from all people that you know, especially your family. You can be a righteous man without being a Jew. In biblical terms we call that *Ger Toshav*, or resident alien. People that do not convert to Judaism, but recognize the universal moral imperative on which our faith is based. According to the Prophet Amos, the moral demands on humanity are universal and all the nations of this world are bound by certain moral laws and are accountable for their conduct. If you follow the basic norms and responsibilities of human conduct, which we call the *Noahide* covenant, you do not have to become a Jew. In contrast, the Jewish people were given at Mount Sinai the collective responsibility to follow God's commands. We are held accountable for our actions, which should contribute to the creation of a just world. God gave us the immense responsibility to complete the work he had begun. We have been given the tools in the form of his commands, and we have to follow them. If you choose to become a Jew, then you also choose to bear this collective responsibility. This, my son, can be tough."

I was astonished by the brevity and clarity of his thoughts – and by the challenge he had thrown my way. Was this what I truly want —to take on the responsibility of being a Jew? Do I have what it takes?

"I have to think about that some more," I answered.

He gave me a big smile.

"Such an answer I'd expected from a wise man, not from a young man. It shows that you are truly considering this decision and not acting impulsively. Please understand that I cannot encourage you to convert. Actually I should discourage you, because Judaism does not proselytize."

Seeing the disappointment in my expression, he continued.

"But I will be your sponsor and accept you as a student. I will decide if and when you are ready to take such a step. This may take a long time. Be patient. I know that you have the capacity to study anything about Judaism. This may promote your intellectual understanding of the Jewish faith, but you need much more than that. You need to internalize the faith, feel it in you and apply it in your daily life. This is a growth process similar to the one you have begun. Now you have to repeat it again and again. You will slowly mature, beginning like a child. I suggest that you seek a Jewish community that will adopt you, and Yaacov can help you with that. You need to study Torah, learn how to pray in order to communicate with God, and learn to be patient. This process will take time, but I will be there for you. Remember, it's not enough to love Israel. You need to embrace the Torah. After the destruction of the Second Temple by the Romans, the Torah, became the centre of Jewish faith. Some call it our 'portable homeland,' the incarnation of our desire to return to Israel. The Torah contains the mission statement of the Jewish people. It's a story empowering people to do God's will and to change the world according to his desire. Do you understand?"

I nodded slowly, beginning to understand the enormity of the tasks that lay ahead.

"Now we have talked enough. Let's have dessert." He obviously wanted me to review and revisit my decision, and I had to accept this, even though I was more impatient than I may have appeared. I wanted guidance and instructions on how to proceed.

Of course he was observing all this.

"You seem to have lost your appetite," he said.

I had to admit to my growing sense of confusion.

"Rabbi, I respect your opinion. Please do not misunderstand me, but I am at a loss about where to go from here."

"Bernd, you have to find yourself first. Complete your studies, obtain your professional degree, give yourself time to grow and mature. Let ethical principals guide your daily life. I don't expect you to be perfect. I want you to understand that it is more important to enjoy the journey toward such goals than to achieve them. A quick conversion will be like a change of clothes. It will change the way you look, but not who you are. We will stay in touch and you will keep me posted about your progress."

Before I could answer he had asked for the check, stood, and prepared to leave.

"Shalom, my young friend, and do not forget. Rome was not built in one day."

I left the restaurant, too, still dazed by the experience. On my way home our conversation replayed in my mind over and over. Yes, he was receptive to my interest to convert, but clearly he wanted me to slow down and to do it on my own. I was young, inexperienced, and impatient. And I felt misunderstood. I though that I already had captured the essence of the belief and knew enough to convert.

But then I remembered his words: I had to internalize the faith and to apply it in my daily life. I realized that he was right, and that this would indeed take time.

The faith I was choosing was only a seedling whose roots needed to be anchored in my life, its growth nurtured by responsible living.

Time was on my side but I had yet to face many challenges.

THE ECLIPSE

STAYING IN A STUDENT dormitory was a challenge. Crammed into small spaces with little privacy, we students had to share everything: kitchen, shower, other facilities. Nevertheless, the crowded quarters provided many opportunities to interact with interesting students from all over the world. Germany was a popular destination for students from the Middle East to study medicine, engineering, and computer sciences.

On my floor lived many Palestinians, Syrians, and Iranians. They all expanded my knowledge of the world. Still, I decided to avoid any disclosure of my interest in Judaism and Israel.

Soon after starting my studies, apparently a new neighbor moved into the room next to me. On that day I found a note from the housekeeper on my door when I returned from classes. It read: *Your mother called to wish you a Happy Birthday.* Beneath it another note, in a different handwriting, said: *And a Happy Birthday From Me. Knock at my door if you want to.*

So I did. Several seconds later a stunning young woman opened the door. She had long black hair, olive skin, and brown eyes.

"Hi, my name is Roberta. I am your new neighbor and want to wish you Happy Birthday, or *Feliz Cumpleaños* as they say in my country."

Her accent and complexion clearly revealed her Latin background, though she was speaking flawless German.

"Thank you. Where are you from?" I asked curiously.

"I am Mexican and study philosophy here," she answered.

Noticing the immediate mutual attraction, I invited her for dinner at a local Mexican restaurant. That same night we not only enjoyed our first dinner, but also discovered and explored our physical desire for each other. Our relationship could be best described as a fireworks of uncontrolled sexuality, which, once ignited, would eventually burn out.

From that moment we were an inseparable couple, surfing a wave of lust and sensuality.

But while we were content for a time to explore our common interests, eventually we also had to face our differences. One of those was her growing displeasure in my interest in Judaism and Israel. During a late-night dinner I shared with her the conflict I had with my father and our growing alienation. Roberta stared at me in disbelief.

"In my culture we respect our parents regardless," she said, unknowingly echoing my own parents' words. "How can you accuse your father of wrongdoing? And if he was involved in any of those crimes against the Jewish people, why do you feel responsible for what happened?"

"Your point is well taken, but let me clarify. I do not blame my father for those crimes committed in Germany's name. I blame him for blindly following orders and accepting authority uncritically. He must have known what was happening, but he chose to ignore it. That's what I blame him for."

"Why do you want to embrace a new religion anyway? As a student of philosophy I subscribe to Karl Marx and his interpretation of religion. Have you heard about it?"

"Well, I do remember that he called religion the opium of the people. Correct?"

"Good. I should have known that you would know that much," she remarked dryly.

"But there is more to that story," and she pulled out a book from her small book shelf and after a short search found the passage she was looking for.

"Let me quote you what he really wrote: "The abolition of religion as the illusory happiness of the people is at the same time the demand for their real happiness. The demand to give up the illusion about their condition is a demand to give up a condition that requires illusions. Criticism has plucked the imaginary flowers from the chains so that man may throw off the chains and pluck the real flowers. Religion is only the illusory sun around which man revolves so long as he does not revolve around himself."

She closed the book and looked at me triumphantly.

"Karl Marx was a Jew and he realized that religion served only one purpose. To justify oppression and to convince people to accept their living conditions. Religion helps the ruling class maintain their power and exploit the common folk."

I leaned backwards to gather my thoughts. I understood her position. It reflected the view of many leftists who called for a religion of liberation.

"Let me try to explain what Judaism really means," I said. "I may agree that one should not interpret the Bible or Torah literally. It actually tells a story about the human condition and how to assume and carry out responsibility. Actually, it represents the history of a people, the Jews, who liberated themselves from slavery, were lead by Moses into freedom and then had the choice to accept God's commands and will. Jews are called upon NOT to accept reality as it is, but to change it according to God's will. Jews do not accept the world as it is, but strive to improve it. Therefore, I cannot agree that Karl Marx's interpretation of religion applies to Judaism."

She looked at me disapprovingly.

"You are an idealistic thinker and dwell in a metaphysical world. I am grounded in the here and now. For me God does not exist and plays no role in my life. I also want to remind you that the State of Israel enslaves and oppresses millions of Palestinians. The Israelis obviously have thrown their religious principals overboard. "

She knew that this kind of talk would anger me, so I tried to control my emotions.

"Did you hear this from the Palestinian students or have you been to Israel and actually visited Palestinian villages as I have?"

"Of course I did not visit Palestine. I do not need too. It's obvious to the whole world that Israel is abusing the Palestinians."

We had reached a point where I either had to stop the discussion or slip into a full-scale verbal altercation.

"I think we should agree that we disagree," I proposed.

"I think we should realize that we are different and may not have a lot in common," she said more bluntly, "except our physical attraction.

I knew deep inside that she was correct, but did not want to accept the truth. From that day our relationship slowly disintegrated. We still saw each other for the satisfaction of our physical needs, but we both realized that we were not meant for each other. I had a difficult time disengaging, and took to drinking to sooth the pain I felt so intensely.

Emotionally I was so attached to her that I neglected my own needs, especially my desire for spirituality.

I realized that I confused our physical attraction with love, a sensation I never really experienced.

I also realized that Rabbi Lieberman may have been right and that I was not ready to convert. Flagellated by self doubt, I slipped deeper into despair and my drinking intensified. I neglected my studies and neglected myself.

I had reached low point in my personal life. I realized that I had to refocus on my spiritual goals, and I returned to Bamberg to meet with Yaacov. He was willing to receive me, but frowned at my appearance.

"What happened young man? You are looking angry and distraught." I shared with him my personal struggles and he listened carefully before answering.

"Bernd, nobody expects you to be perfect. Look, the people of Israel wandered in the desert for forty years before they reached the promised land. And then Moses, their leader, did not enter the land with them. Do you know why?" I shook my head.

"Even by foot one can cross the Sinai desert from Egypt to Israel within several weeks or a few months. We don't know if it really took forty years and it doesn't matter. What is important to God was that his chosen people were not ready to embrace his commandments, and they went astray. They worshiped idols and sought pleasure. You have to understand that the human condition has not changed much in the last few thousand years, even though we have changed the way we live and the environment we live in. Your behavior is no exception. You sought immediate gratification and indulged in earthly pleasures. Deep inside you knew you were wrong, and you used alcohol to desensitize yourself. Yes, I agree. You are not ready. But you have the ability to change, and I will be here to help. Now go home and get some rest. Come back once you are ready to learn."

I felt deeply ashamed, but also gratified that I could share my feelings and thoughts with him. I returned to the student dormitory and promised myself to refocus. I knew I could move forward and needed to gather my inner strength.

I followed Yaacov's advice and attended Friday night services at the synagogue in nearby Nuremberg. The first time, I went I was reluctant to join the synagogue because I felt that the presence of a non-Jew would be inappropriate and even disrespectful. As I entered the synagogue, a man wearing a dark cape and a black hat greeted me. He had a wide face with soft features and shook my hand vigorously.

"Shabbat Shalom. My name is Mr. Kanowitz and I am the cantor. Where are you from?"

I tried to respond to his firm handshake, but my anxiety was palpable.

"My name is Bernd. Yaacov Eisenberg from Bamberg referred me here."

He smiled.

"Yes, yes, I know Yaacov. A good man with a great heart. Please come in and join us for the service."

I was struck by the friendly reception and my anxiety slowly abated. Still, being unfamiliar with the liturgy of the Jewish prayer services, I chose to sit in the back.

Soon many more people arrived, especially elderly man and women from the nearby Jewish old age home. I noticed also a few younger faces in the gathering crowd.

After a few minutes of loud talking and laughter, the cantor approached the podium and everybody stood up. Then he began singing in a baritone voice,

"*L'khah dodi liq'rat kalah p'nei Shabbat n'qab'lah,* Come out my beloved, the bride, to meet; the inner light of Shabbat, let us greet."

I closed my eyes and the melody carried me away back to Jerusalem. I felt the same emotions I had felt at the Western Wall. The same spiritual energy engulfed me and I immersed myself in the prayer.

"*Adonai echad ush'mo echad L'Shem ul'tif'eret v'lit'hilah,* God is One and His Name is One, for renown, for glory and in song."

When the cantor stopped, I was transformed in the spirit of the *Kabbalat Shabbat,* acceptance of the Shabbat. At that moment, I felt one with all those present. My anxiety and fears disappeared.

After the service, the cantor walked toward me and shook my hand again.

"Come back again. Please come back again. I know that you will find what you are looking for."

I looked at him in surprise.

"How do you know what I am looking for?"

"Well, first of all, our Jewish world here is small, and word travels fast when a stranger joins us. Yaacov had already told me about you so I knew immediately who you were when you walked through the door. I observed you during the service and I noticed that prayer touches your heart. Come back and you will discover the spiritual energy within you. I know you will come back."

He was right. I would come back again many times.

That night I returned to the student dormitory, and as I unlocked my door I saw Roberta entering the hallway.

"Where have you been? I was looking for you? Aren't you interested in spending time with me?"

"I was in Nuremberg attending the Jewish Shabbat services."

She curled her lips.

"Since when do you prefer prayer over sex? Are the Jews turning you on now? "

Her blunt and direct response filled me with anger.

"One has nothing to do with the other. You know that."

"No, I do not know it. Show me what you mean."

Feeling challenged and hurt I grabbed her hand and pulled her toward me.

"Don't talk to me like that ever again," I yelled.

She smiled and kissed me on the mouth.

"I love it when you explode in anger. Use it and give it to me."

After spending the night with her, I rose early, feeling disgusted with myself, and went for a walk. It was still dark, the sunrise hours away. I had to stop this destructive behavior, this terrible attraction. Yes, I was a young man seeking pleasure with her, but I was also a spiritual seeker, and could not be both at once. When I was honest with myself, I knew that our relationship was superficial and often mutually abusive. I was ashamed of my indecision and weakness, especially when I compared my behavior with the dedication of the spiritual leaders I had had the good fortune to meet.

Why could I not gather my strength and reach a decision and part from her?

I returned to my room and lay in bed with my eyes wide open, waiting for morning. By the time morning came, I knew what I had to do. I got up, packed my suitcase, and left. I spent the next week in a hotel, then returned to the dormitory to gather the remainder of my few belongings. Entering my room I found a handwritten note slipped under the door. In a few pointed sentences Roberta wrote that she had left for Mexico to visit her parents and that I could contact her there.

I longed for her, but at the same time I yearned for my freedom. I decided to call my father that afternoon. My parents had recently moved back to Bamberg and purchased a house in the suburbs that was adjacent to a picturesque castle and had a magnificent view over the entire city.

He picked up the receiver, and despite his attempt to conceal his emotions, I heard that he was relieved to hear my voice.

"We haven't heard from you for months and I guess you are in trouble, otherwise you wouldn't call," he remarked in his dry way.

"I need a place to sort out my affairs," I conceded. "So far I have not been too successful. Can I return home for a while?"

"Your mother will be pleased to see you," he answered.

We had played this game before, and I avoided the temptation to ask him if he would be pleased as well. The same day I returned to Bamberg and moved into a small ground-floor apartment. A separate entrance gave me some privacy from my parents in the house overhead.

This was a difficult move for me. I felt as though I had failed and again required my parent's support. Yet I could not bring myself to share my pain and struggle with my father.

I decided I needed a strict structure for my days, following a disciplined schedule of exercise and work, and attending religious services at the synagogues in Bamberg and Nuremberg. Commuting daily by train to the university, I often returned home late at night without seeing my parents.

Several months later Roberta returned from Mexico. She contacted me several times. Despite my determination, I could not resist the temptation of casual physical encounters. But when she told me that she was going to move back to Mexico in the summer, I was relieved. I was unable or unwilling to sever all ties with her, but she made the decision for me.

That summer, political tensions escalated in the Middle East. On June 3, 1982, the Israeli ambassador in the United Kingdom was assaulted by three members of a Palestinian radical faction, sustaining severe injuries that left him comatose and paralyzed. Several days later, the Israeli army invaded Lebanon to wipe out the operational bases of militant Palestinian groups. Defense minister Ariel Sharon ordered the Israel Defense Forces to strike deep into Lebanon and to move toward the capital of Beirut, and the Israeli artillery and air force bombarded and shelled the city for weeks. Christian Lebanese President Bashir Gemayel was assassinated, and the Lebanese Christian militia, which was allied with Israel, entered two Palestinian refugee camps and massacred hundreds of civilians. Israeli troops allegedly surrounded the camps with tanks and troops, responding to Christian militia intelligence reports that several thousand armed Palestinian fighters were holed up in the camps.

The massacre was blamed not only on the Christian militia seeking revenge for the killing of their leader, but on Israel, which was held responsible for not intervening in the cruel massacre of innocent women and children. News of the war and the subsequent massacre of Palestinian civilians triggered massive protests in Germany, especially by the left-wing parties and the Palestinian student union, whose leaders were supported and trained in Communist East Germany. Israeli flags were burned daily during student protests, and soon Jews and Jewish institutions were targeted. Synagogues had to be protected by heavily armed police and it was increasingly difficult for me and others to attend religious services.

Soon I became personally involved. Palestinian students organized a forum discussion in the main auditorium of the University in Erlangen. They accused Israel of war crimes and called for a Nuremberg-style trial. Most speakers were very articulate Palestinians, skilled at whipping the audience into a frenzy.

"Who are the enemies?" One speaker screamed.

"The Israelis!" the crowd roared.

"Who kills innocent women and children?"

"The Israelis!!"

"Who is responsible for repression and war in the world?"

"The Israelis!!!"

"Who controls the banks and the media?"

"The Israelis!!!!!"

By then the German students were on their feet screaming. Faces red and eyes bloodshot, they appeared ready to follow any command. The speaker was fully aware that he was in control and asked everyone to sit down. At that point I gathered my strength and stood up.

"Aren't you ashamed of yourselves! This city is located just a few miles from the arena where Adolf Hitler spewed his anti-Semitic propaganda. Forty years later Germans again blame Jews for all the misery in the world. Aren't we supposed to learn from our parent's mistakes?"

The crowd fell silent, and only one person looked at me. It was Roberta, sitting in the first row and staring in surprise.

One of the Palestinian speakers, a tall muscular man with curly black hair who reminded me of Chalid, immediately responded.

"He must be a Jew. Don't listen to him! He wants to use the Holocaust to make you feel guilty. Now we Palestinians are the victims and the Jews the perpetrators. After the Second World War the Jews came from Europe to Palestine and took away our land, claiming that they were displaced by the Holocaust. They killed our women and children and evicted millions of us. Now we Palestinians suffer because your parents killed the Jews. We suffer from that mistake and now you can make it right again. Support us in our struggle."

This time the crowd did not roar in agreement, but waited on my response. I looked at Roberta, then at the audience. Most avoided eye contact with me.

"Two wrongs don't make a right. Supporting the hateful anti-Semitic propaganda you heard today from these paid agitators won't remove the responsibility we have as Germans toward the Jewish people. No, we should not uncritically support everything the Israeli government is doing, but we should act on the facts. Today all of you have acted like our parents or grandparents who supported

Hitler. You stopped asking questions and repeated the propaganda presented to you. You are no better than they were. You have no reason to criticize them."

Meanwhile, several muscular Palestinians approached me from behind and before I could continue they grabbed me by the shoulder, pulled me to the exit, and threw me out the door.

"Go back where you came from, you dirty Jew," one of them screamed and went back into the building.

I straightened out my jacket and was about to leave when I heard Roberta's voice.

"Are you okay? Why are you getting involved? This is not your calling.

The Palestinians are trying to educate us about their suffering."

I looked at her and tried unsuccessfully to control my anger.

"You know what the difference is between you and me? I stand up for what I believe in and I say what I think needs to be said. You are just like the other sheep in that crowd, repeating phrases, not realizing that you are being manipulated."

She stared defiantly at me with her dark yet beautiful eyes.

"Nobody will listen to you. Go back to your books and prayers. Find yourself a Jewish girlfriend and go on with your life."

She turned and followed my Palestinian tormenters into the auditorium.

I don't know which hurt more, my physical or emotional bruises.

That evening, I returned to my parents' home and was surprised to see them still up, sitting in the living room watching the news. My father noticed my return and called to me.

"Have you seen what is happening in Lebanon?"

I knew what he was referring too, and braced myself for another volley of insults.

"You should have seen the TV reports about the massacre in the Palestinian refugee camps. Your Jews have killed thousands of innocent Palestinians. They have created their own Holocaust now!"

Almost victoriously he went on, "now don't you recognize that Jews are no better then anybody else? At least we Germans have learned from our mistakes, whereas the Jews cynically use the Holocaust to blame us Germans and extract money from us."

My mother sat silently at the table, nervously sipping a glass of wine. Her cheeks were flushed from alcohol and her eyes bloodshot.

I did not want to respond to my father's provocation, but I couldn't resist asking the same question I had asked so many times before.

"What have YOU learned from the past? Tell me! Did you turn in your medals after the war, recognizing that you fought for a tyrant? Did you realize that those who tried to assassinate Hitler were not committing treason, but trying to rid Germany of a dictator? Did you speak up when ex-Nazis rose in the ranks of post-war Germany?"

My father looked at me, his lips pressed tightly together. Fists clenched, he stood and approached me with an unsteady gait.

"I expect an apology from you. I am still your father and I demand your respect!!"

"Father," I answered. "You can regain my respect and trust by leveling with me. Tell me the truth about your past. Share with me your thoughts. Remember our long walks on Sunday mornings? We were talking all the time. You always listened to me and I learned so much from you. I admired you and deep in my heart I still do."

Despite his drunkenness, my words seemed to have touched him. His tight expression seemed to soften, but only for a few seconds.

"Son, we have so little in common any more. You have decided to pursue your own life. Find your own ways. You have to learn that you will walk this path on your own. Don't expect us to help you. I will let you live here, because your mother asked me to. Otherwise, you would be on the street. It was, and still is, your choice."

Then he turned around, walked up the steps to his study, and, as he had done all his life, closed the door.

My mother had sat silent during the entire conversation. When I looked at her she had tears in her eyes.

"Why are you doing this to yourself? Why are you doing this to us? You could have such a good life?"

Standing in front of her I stroked her hair and touched her hand.

"Because I have found something in me that I thought I never possessed. I am searching for more than money or possessions. I am searching for truth, inner peace, and happiness. That's all I want. It is up to you two to accept me the way I am, instead of the way you want me to be."

She took my hand and pressed it hard.

"Do what you have to do. I will take care of your father."

A tear ran down my face as I kissed her good-night. I wished she could have been stronger, or maybe that I should have been. During the following weeks the political turmoil at the university subsided and I could focus on my medical training and study of Judaism. Several times I saw Roberta at the university library, and we succeeded in ignoring each other, except for one time. I was sitting at a table studying when she approached me.

"Hi, how are you," she said softly.

I smiled at her but was reluctant to answer.

"Fine," I finally said.

"I just want to apologize for my behavior the last time we met. I must say I admire your commitment to follow your convictions. I am sorry it did not work out between us."

I listened to her carefully.

"Why are you saying that now?"

"Because tonight I leave town and fly back to Mexico tomorrow morning. I wanted to make peace before I leave. We will probably never see each other again."

My throat went dry and I almost choked when I tried to answer.

"I want to thank you for having the courage to speak to me, and I wish you the best. Only health and happiness."

Tears ran down her face as she embraced me for the last time.

"Take care of yourself my stubborn German friend. I know you will leave for Israel and please stay safe."

We stood for a minute in a silent embrace, then she pushed herself away. For months after her departure I avoided places where we spent time together. I tried unsuccessfully to sweep her memory from my mind. But finally, as time passed, my realization strengthened that I had to go on with my life, to pursue my career and my dream.

My determination to convert was strong, and my focus on this path was clear.

Now I needed to prove that I was mature enough to take the final steps.

CHAPTER 4

THE CONVERSION

RABBI LIEBERMAN MAILED ME a Torah and Talmud assignment every other week. Never having studied the Torah, the five books of Moses, or the Talmud, the rabbinic discussion of Jewish law and ethics, I was forced to pay close attention to their contents and to the ancient Hebrew language, which I did not learn until later.

When my father intercepted one of these packages, he opened it and left it on the kitchen table. He never asked me about its contents, or why I was interested in studying religious texts. Following this incident, the rabbi followed my request to address the packages to the Jewish Community in Bamberg, where I picked them up.

I attended Friday night services in the synagogue in Nuremberg, and the cantor invited me to join the subsequent dinner receptions. In the beginning most attendees paid little attention to my presence, but during subsequent dinners, I was approached on several occasions. My youthful appearance triggered immediate questions about my marital status, and once identified as a single young man, the matchmakers began trying to introduce me to single Jewish women. I knew that matchmaking, or *shidduch,* was part of Jewish tradition, but I was surprised that nobody asked me whether I was Jewish to begin with.

I was not yet ready for a partner, arranged or otherwise. Witnessing my obvious predicament, the Cantor approached me.

"Why are you so reluctant to consider an offer to marry?"

"You know I cannot. I am not even Jewish."

He looked at me and smiled.

"Since I first met you, you have grown a beard, and your complexion is that of a Jew. Most people here would never suspect you were German unless you told them. You appear so serious and involved in the prayer service that even I would think you were a Jew."

He was correct. Not only had I changed my outward appearance, but the study of the Torah and Talmud deeply touched me and changed my character and heart. I discovered the universality of the call for individual and collective responsibility. I also understood that we do not have to defer salvation to a paradise to come, but can contribute our daily share of small actions to improving the world today.

"Do you think I am ready, Cantor, to take the final step?"

"Only you can answer that question. If you believe that God exists and communicates with us. If you believe that God made a covenant with the people of Israel at Mount Sinai, and that we are bound by this covenant to follow his commands. Then and only then you are ready to consider. Are you ready?"

I looked at him and closed my eyes for a moment. I opened them and said,

"Yes, I am. Yes, I am."

He smiled and hugged me.

"*KolHaKavod*, all respect. I am proud of you. I will contact Yaacov in Bamberg and Rabbi Lieberman. You will hear from them. Be patient. The day will come."

Months passed. I continued to attend services and Jewish holiday celebrations. Even though I was not obligated to fast on the Day of Atonement, I did so, and requested absence from my medical school classes when holiday services conflicted with my studies.

Still, as a non-Jew, I was not allowed to be called for the Saturday morning Torah readings and was not counted as a member for a minyan.

One day in late October, I received a phone call from Yaacov asking me for a favor, but he was unwilling to discuss it on the phone. He sounded distressed so I left immediately to meet him at his office. When I arrived at the Jewish community center in Bamberg,

I heard a loud argument in Yiddish coming from his office. I found him sitting with three other elderly men, but could not yet fully understand what they were saying. Noticing my arrival, everybody except Yaacov felt silent.

"Come in, Bernd, and please sit down."

I noticed the tense atmosphere, and the three other men, whom I never met, looked at me suspiciously.

"Bernd, we have a serious matter. One of our members died and we are in need of able-bodied men to bury him."

Recognizing my bafflement, he continued.

"In our tradition we cannot just call an undertaker. Once a Jew dies we have to follow certain rules and steps, and for that we have a *chevra kadisha*, or burial society. Unfortunately, we have only a few able-bodied men in our dwindling community, and you see them before you. We need your help."

At that moment one of the old men stood up. He was thin and wore an ill-fitting jacket. His face was pale and the few remaining streaks of hair on his head were white. Only his eyes reflected an unbroken spirit, and once he began to speak I realized that his was the voice that was leading the loud arguments when I arrived.

"Young man, my name is Abraham. I survived Auschwitz and I never thought I would have to ask a German for help in burying a fellow member. I heard that you are serious young man who is converting to Judaism. Is that correct?"

I nodded silently.

"You are also a medical student and have knowledge of the human anatomy."

"Yes," I responded. "I am going to finish medical school soon. But why is that important?"

"Because as a member of the chevrah kadisha you need to be able to clean and prepare the body for burial, and not many men can do that. Are you ready to help us?"

I looked into the eyes of four old men who were torn between their commitment to their tradition and their horrific experience with Germans during the Holocaust. I could see the pain it caused them to ask a German to assist them in this private and sacred act.

"Yes, of course I will help. Please let me know what to do."

Abraham looked at Yaacov and the other men in the room. They all nodded silently and then one after the other stood up and shook my hand. By some tacit process they had come to a difficult agreement to accept my assistance and help.

"My name is Hershel," said one, and the last introduced himself as Zelig.

"Do you have anything scheduled for today?" Yaacov asked. "We have to start now, because the funeral will be tomorrow morning."

"Now?" I blurted out, remembering seconds later that tonight my parents were having a family dinner celebrating their wedding anniversary. For my father, my attendance was mandatory.

"Any plans for tonight?" Yaavov inquired.

"Nothing that can't wait," I lied, accepting that my absence would cause a major conflict with my family.

I was torn between my obligation to my family and the request to assist with the burial preparation.

"So, what do you want to do? " Yaacov asked.

"I will come with you to help," I answered.

Minutes later I found myself in the back of an old Mercedes seated between Herschel and Zelig. Nobody spoke during the drive to the Jewish cemetery. When we arrived, the caretaker opened the gate of the small Jewish burial home. We slowly entered an old one-story building where a German family lived. This family had for many years diligently and passionately cared for the small but growing cemetery, which was separated by a wall from the larger Christian section of the cemetery. I remembered now that many years prior I had visited the grave of my grandparents, which was located on the other side of the wall and just a stone's throw away from it.

We were shown into a large room with a mortician's table in the center. On the table lay a body covered with a plastic sheet.

"Cover yourself with the yarmulke," Abraham said, placing a black skullcap on my head.

Reciting a prayer, Herschel and Zelig removed the plastic sheets revealing the emaciated body of a man who had obviously succumbed to cancer.

"We must thoroughly cleanse the skin, and then ritually clean him with a continuous flow of water," Yaacov said. "The process is called *Tahara*, or ritual purification. Afterward we have to dry the body and dress him in *tachrichim*, or white garments."

"What are those garments for?" I asked.

"They symbolize the garments the High Priests wore in the Temple in Jerusalem. Afterward we have to place the body in a wooden casket, even though Jewish tradition calls for open burial, which is used in Israel. This is prohibited in Germany, and we have to follow the law."

Despite the freezing temperatures we removed our jackets and shirts and wore short-sleeved plastic overcoats to wash the body. At that moment I noticed that every member of the chevrah kadisha but me had a number tattooed on his right forearm. Herschel and Zelig noticed me staring at their numbers.

"Don't worry, "Zelig said. "It's not your fault. I am glad you are helping us."

I was deeply moved by his words. Then Herschel placed a hand on my shoulder.

"You are one of us now. Yaacov told me about you, and I had a hard time believing what he said. Now I see that you are truly following your heart."

We continued silently and with the utmost respect to clean the deceased, following a strict sequence of procedures. We washed the head first, then the right side, the left side, the front, and the back. I was given a large wooden toothpick to cleanse toenails and fingernails.

"Jews believe one should be clean and pure when judged by God," Herschel said. "This is why we pay such attention to detail."

Once the body was cleansed and dried, Abraham opened small packets of earth and sprinkled them on the eyes, heart, and genitals.

"Why is he doing that?" I asked Yaacov.

"These are soil samples from Israel, representing the Holy Land, and we place them on those organs that are viewed as the source of all sin."

We placed white linen garments over the head, torso, legs, and feet, then lifted the body into a simple pine box and closed the coffin without using nails. Once finished we all stood silently in front of the coffin.

"There are no family members available to say Kaddish," Zelig remarked. I understood that the Kaddish, or Mourners' Prayer for the Dead, has to be recited by a family member to honor the deceased. In the absence of any family, it was up to us to say the prayer. The prayer is written in Aramaic, which in ancient times was a common language among Jews.

"*Yitgaddal v'yitqaddash sh'meh rabba,* exalted and sanctified is God's great name," Zelig began by heart. "*B' al'ma d'hu atid l'itchaddata ul achaya metaya ul assaqa yathon l'chayyey al'ma,* in the world which will be renewed and He will give life to the dead and raise them to eternal life," the others responded.

"Help us my friend to honor the dead," Zelig said, smiling at me. I understood his intent and without hesitation I joined them in prayer. "*Ulmivne qarta dirushlem ulshakhlala hekhleh b'gavvah ulme qar pulchana nukhra a m'ar a v'la atava pulchana dishmayya l'atreh,* and rebuild the city of Jerusalem and establish his temple within, removing foreign worship from the earth, and the Heavenly service shall return."

At that moment I remembered the prayer I had heard as a young boy on television after the arrival of the coffins of the murdered Israeli Olympic athletes in Tel Aviv. I now understood that it was the Kaddish that had touched me so deeply.

I now felt as one with this group of Jewish men paying respect to a deceased community member. The prayer detached me from the here-and-now, and I felt transformed into a timeless entity. After several minutes of silence, Yaacov touched my arm.

"Let's go. Without you we could not have finished this task, and I want to thank you for that. Abraham, Herschel, and Zelig will remain here tonight to watch over the body, and I will drop you off at your house. You need to go home now." He didn't know how far removed from home I felt.

When I arrived at my parents' house, my father heard me and a short while later he entered my room. I was still wearing my yarmulke and had a prayer book in my hand to finish the evening prayer.

His face turned red at the sight and he screamed at me.

"I cannot believe it! With your beard and stupid skullcap you even look like a Jew. Why are you doing this to your self? Why are you doing this to us?"

"I am doing what I feel and know is right for me."

My answer did not satisfy him and he continued.

"Don't tell me that you missed an important family event because you had more important cult-related issues to attend too?"

I closed my eyes seeking an answer that would not infuriate him.

"I am sorry that I missed the dinner. Yes, I had a very urgent matter to attend to."

I was reluctant to share my experience with him because I knew that it would further aggravate an already bad situation. His abrupt answer did not surprise me.

"You have to decide where you want to go. Stay here, or join your Jews." He left my room, slamming the door behind him.

My father was right, and so was the cantor and Yaacov. They all agreed that I had to decide what to do, and now I knew what to do.

The next day I attended the emotional funeral with the few community members who came together to honor the dead. Yaacov gave a short speech honoring the memory of the deceased, Cantor Kanowitz from Nuremberg recited the Kaddish, and afterwards we returned to the synagogue for a meal. As I approached Yaacov and the Cantor, my expression had already revealed to them that I had a serious matter to discuss.

"I am ready to go ahead with the conversion!" I blurted out.

After a moment of silence, Yaacov answered:

"In order to proceed, you have to undergo a circumcision, immerse yourself in a ritual bath, and appear before a rabbinical court to demonstrate that you accept and understand the obligations of being an observant Jew. I will contact Rabbi Lieberman today to get his approval. You have to understand that all of those procedures have to be supervised by a witness determined appropriate by the rabbinical court. That means that you may have to travel to different places to comply with those rules."

I nodded in agreement.

"So be it, and I will wait for your answer," I replied.

"My son, what do you want to do when you have completed the

conversion?" the cantor asked.

"I have thought about that issue for a long time. In two months I will graduate from medical school and then I have to complete my civil service commitment, which I deferred. Instead, I will emigrate to Israel, join the Israeli Army, and serve that country."

Yaacov and the cantor looked at me in disbelief.

"We thought that you may stay here to revive our community," the cantor said.

"Please understand. I am a young man. My relationship with my family is failing and I do not want to live here and later lament the fact that I never tried to pursue my dreams. Since the first time I set foot in Israel I fell in love with that country and all of its contradictions. I want at least to try living there."

"I don't think that we can stop you,

"Yaacov remarked with disappointment.

"I miss you already and hope that you will succeed. I will let you know tomorrow about the rabbi's decision."

I eagerly awaited his answer and the next day in the afternoon I waited in the synagogue. Several hours passed, and finally Yaacov emerged from his office and handed me an envelope. "I just got off the phone after speaking with the rabbi. He had many questions, and asked me all about your behavior and character. I answered them all. He then dictated a detailed list of tasks you have to complete."

I opened the envelope and reviewed the list. It did not contain any surprises, but I was concerned that I had to leave Germany to undergo the circumcision and the ritual bath and to meet the strict requirements of the rabbinical court. Among Germany's few surviving Jews almost no community offered such services and the available ritual baths were not certified or supervised.

The Rabbi recommended that I contact a *mohel*, a person ordained to do ritual circumcision under the guidelines of the Jewish religion, in Basel, Switzerland, and a rabbi in Metz, France, who was qualified to supervise my immersion in a ritual bath or *mikvah*. These journeys presented practical problems. As a medical student I had limited financial means, and I also had to prepare for my final exams. I decided to go ahead anyway. I sold everything I had and borrowed the rest of the money from Yaacov, who volunteered to help me.

After setting up the appointments, I traveled by car to Basel where I arrived on a Thursday afternoon and checked into a local hospital. I was greeted by Dr. Dan Ruben, a medical doctor and mohel who explained the procedure and advised me to do it under general anesthesia. He offered to answer any questions, and I asked what problems I might expect after the procedure.

He looked at me with a serious face.

"At times we have to physically adjust the male convert to meet the requirements to join the Jewish people." Noticing my concerned look, he grinned and laughed at his joke. "Don't worry. You will be just fine."

After he left the room, I went through pre-operative screening and then was left alone with my thoughts. I was convinced that I was doing the right thing, but wished I had family or friends around me. Still, it was my decision now, and I had to take the final steps by myself.

The next morning I was prepped for the surgery and wheeled into the operating room. On the operating table, the nurse inserted the needle for anesthesia. Just before she began, the mohel entered the room.

"Bernd, you won't be conscious during the procedure and therefore I want to begin the prayers now. Are you ready?" I nodded. He closed his eyes and held my hand.

"Praised be Thou, O Lord, our God, King of the Universe, who hast sanctified us with Thy commandments, and commanded us concerning the rite of circumcision. Praised by Thou, O Lord our God, King of the Universe, who has sanctified us by Thy commandments, and hast bidden us to make him enter into the covenant of Abraham our father."

He stopped and opened his eyes.

"Bernd, have you chosen a Hebrew name? I can enter it on your certificate of circumcision."

I took a deep breath and then answered.

"Yes, I have. My chosen name will be Dov, the bear."

"Ah, the origin of the German name Bernd is bear, too. Good choice."

He continued with the prayer,

"Creator of the universe. May it be Thy gracious will to regard and accept this circumcision, as if I had brought this man before Thy glorious throne. And Thou, in Thy abundant mercy, through Thy holy angels, give a pure and holy heart to Dov, the son of Arthur, who will now be circumcised in honor of Thy great Name. May his heart be wide open to comprehend Thy holy Law, that he may learn and teach, keep and fulfill Thy laws."

Already I felt the tingling sensation of the anesthetic running through my vein and my eyes quickly closed.

Several hours later I woke up to find the mohel standing next to me.

"Mazel tov, congratulations. You now have taken the first step towards completing your conversion. I want you to stay for the night and have Shabbat dinner with us."

"I am sorry, but I can't. My family doesn't know I am here and I'd better get back home before I am missed."

"You shouldn't travel, at least not right now," he admonished me.

"I understand and truly appreciate your concerns, but I have to leave. It's better that way."

That same afternoon I paid the charges and left the hospital against medical advice. I arrived early the next morning and, overcome by fatigue, I fell asleep on my bed, after barely managing to change my wound dressing. In the early afternoon I woke up, refreshed myself, and was about to leave the house when my father stopped me at the door.

"What happened to you? You were gone for almost two days. Your mother was worried sick and then we found bloody bandages in the garbage. I demand an answer now!"

He stared at me with a furious look. I felt literally cornered.

"I am converting to Judaism and took the first step toward that."

His mouth dropped opened and his face broke into disbelief. When he could speak again his voice was one of anger, despair, and fear.

"You have let them mutilate you just to be able to join this cult? Are you out of your mind? I cannot recognize in you the son I raised. Why? Why? What did I do wrong?"

I tried to answer him as best as I could at that moment.

"Actually, you did nothing wrong. Your actions, behavior and demeanor triggered my curiosity and you always fostered my insatiable appetite for answers to so many open questions. I searched and found those answers in Judaism. It's too late, father. I have determined how I want to live my life. We drifted apart a long time ago and now I have to go my own way."

At that moment I thought I might have seen tears in my father's eyes, but within a split second his face turned red and he screamed.

"Get out of my house! Get out of here now!"

He opened the door and I stepped out before he threw it shut. So much for honesty, I thought, but at least I had acknowledged my secrets and set myself free.

I moved to a local motel to recover. I had to focus on my final exams the following month. Throwing myself back into work allowed me to distract myself from the painful disintegration of my relationship with my father.

Three weeks later, I had to interrupt my studies and travel to France for the immersion in the ritual bath or Mikveh. The directions guided me to the outskirts of a small French village outside the city of Metz. There I was met at an old and nondescript building by a French rabbi, who wore a bushy white beard, a broad-rimmed black hat, and a long black coat.

"*Bon après-midi*, good afternoon. I expected you earlier," he said in a soft voice.

"I apologize, but I was not sure where I was going," I said in halting French.

"Let's start with the ceremony," he said. He opened a door that lead into a mid-sized room almost filled by a small pool fed by an underground spring.

"My son, are all of your wounds completely healed? Do you have any open wounds? Otherwise, we have to wait until they are healed to avoid spoiling the water."

He asked me to undress and inspected my body for completeness.

"Yes, you are now ready," he said.

Having studied the instructions, I entered the mikveh, took a deep breath, immersed completely, and remained under water for a few moments. Then I stood, took a breath, and said the blessing:

"*Barukh atah Adonai Eloheinu melekh Ha'olam, asher Kidshanu b'mitzvotav v'tzivanu al ha-tvilah,* Blessed are you, Eternal God, ruler of the universe, who sanctifies us through mitzvot and has enjoined us concerning immersion."

I repeated the immersion a second time, stood, and said:

"*Barukh atah Adonai, Eloheinu melekh Ha'olam, sheh-hecheyanu, v'kiy'manu, v'higianu, la-zman ha-zeh,* Blessed is the Eternal, the God of all creation, who has blessed me with life, sustained me, and enabled me to reach this moment."

For the third and last time I sank beneath the surface, and afterwards recited:

"*Shema Yisrael, Adonal Eloheynu, Adonai echad, Hear, O Israel. The Lord is our God; the Lord is one.!*"

I dressed and the rabbi congratulated me with a big smile.

"Mazel tov, Good luck. I am very happy for you. Here, take this certificate to Germany for the rabbinical court."

Shortly after that I was again on the road, heading back to Germany to appear before the court. I had already forwarded all documents pertaining to the circumcision and immediately received a date to appear before the court – just a few days before my final exams.

THE RABBINICAL COURT

FINALLY, THE APPEARANCE BEFORE the Rabbinical Court, for which I had waited so long was upon me. I was so anxious and excited that I hardly slept the night before I was to leave. The hearing before the Rabbinical Court was scheduled to take place in the city of Trier, a long road trip from Bamberg. Trier is one of the oldest cities in southwest Germany, close to the border of Luxembourg, Conquered by the Romans almost two thousand years ago Roman architecture brought the city new elegance, and even today the proud remnants of the local amphitheater, Roman baths and city gate provide an historic flair comparable to that of Jerusalem.

I left in the wee hours of the morning and arrived at noon, just an hour before my scheduled appearance. The meeting took place in a nondescript old building which had housed a Jewish community dating back to the first century now reduced to a few dozen members.

I walked through an open door and up the stairs leading to a small room. The room was marked with a sign written in Hebrew: Beit HaDin, The Rabbinical Court.

Nobody but me was waiting, and still I did not know how and when I would be called.

So many thoughts raced through my mind. Do I have enough knowledge of Jewish history? Can I recite all the prayers? Will I be accepted despite my family history?

Suddenly, the door opened and Rabbi Lieberman appeared. He smiled and embraced me.

"I have heard many things indicating your readiness. Don't be nervous. Let's go in and have a talk." He gently pushed me into a large, windowless room where two other rabbis sat at each side of a U-shaped table. Both were dressed in dark suits and wore large-brimmed black hats.

Rabbi Lieberman presented me.

"This is our candidate I have talked so much about." Then he turned to me. "Let me introduce you to Rabbi Leibowitz on your right and Rabbi Ben Asher to your left."

"Please sit down young man," Rabbi Leibowitz said. He had a short gray beard and thick eyeglasses and I guessed him to be in his late fifties. Rabbi Ben Asher was studying the file folder containing my application, which seemed to be remarkably voluminous. Then I remembered all the letters I had sent to Rabbi Lieberman and the references he had requested almost every year from people in the Jewish community who knew me.

Rabbi Ben Asher finally looked up and inspected my face. His eyes were gray and he had bushy eyebrows and a large white beard, making it difficult to guess his age. Meanwhile, Rabbi Lieberman sat down at the front table and pointed to a chair placed in front of him.

"Please sit down and let's begin."

He opened his folder and browsed through some of the files.

"I have carefully reviewed all the documents that were submitted on your behalf by different sources, most of them from the Jewish community in Bamberg, personal letters of recommendation, and our own correspondence. I forwarded all the material to the esteemed rabbis present and we got a pretty complete picture of who you are, or at least how you are perceived. Most references attest to the fact that you are truly committed to the Jewish faith and life and are mature enough to make this decision. Please describe in your own words how you found your way to the Jewish faith."

As I had done many times before, I described my life and spiritual journey. After I had finished, all three rabbis remained silent for several minutes. Rabbi Ben Asher broke the silence first.

"I was very impressed by your honest and personal description of your upbringing and your relationship with your father. I understand that he was a Nazi officer."

"He was a Wehrmacht officer, rabbi," I said.

"What's the difference?" he asked.

"As far as I know, he never joined the Nazi party. He felt that it was his duty to serve his country, and especially to follow the military tradition of his family. I think it's important that he realized that his commitment to his country was abused and that he had served a demon. Unfortunately, he has only partially dealt with the past and prefers to conceal the inconvenient and often terrible truth. If he had been a Nazi, I would have had an easier time hating him."

"Do you hate your father?"

"No, I don't. But I never understood his refusal to answer my questions about the past."

"What is it about the past that you are interested in?"

"The truth. The honest truth about why almost everyone looked the other way when they came for the Jews."

"Did you choose to convert as a reaction to your father's omissions or actions or even guilt?"

I paused for a second.

"In the beginning those feelings may have motivated me, but later, and especially after my visit to Israel, I was deeply touched by the Jewish faith and its message."

"What is the message?" Rabbi Leibowitz asked.

I turned toward him.

"To conduct oneself according to the spirit of the commandments and by doing so, translate God's words into action, transforming words into deeds. "

"Are you aware that as a convert you commit yourself to follow the six hundred and thirteen commandments, also called Mitzvot in Hebrew?"

"Yes Rabbi I am aware of that responsibility."

"Tell me, what prayer has touched you the most?"

I answered without hesitation.

"The Kaddish."

"Why the Kaddish?" he asked.

"Because it was the fist prayer I ever heard."

I told him the story of the Olympic massacre in Munique in 1972 and how the images and prayers of the days following those tragic events were burned into my mind.

My description of the events visibly moved him and I later learned that he personally knew the family of one of the murdered athletes.

"Can you recite a prayer in Hebrew? For example the Amidah?"

Of course I was familiar with the Amidah. It is considered the central prayer of the Jewish liturgy. Its name means "standing" in Hebrew, and that is how it is recited. It originally consisted of eighteen blessings and is therefore also known by the Hebrew word for eighteen, *shemoneh esreh*, even though a nineteenth prayer was added later.

"What blessing shall I recite?" I asked.

"The fourth blessing young man. Petition for knowledge and insight, *Da'at* in Hebrew. You remember?"

I nodded, stood up, closed my eyes, and began.

"*Atah chonen leadam data umelamed,* You show favor to a man of knowledge, and you teach understanding to a mortal man. Be gracious to us; a mind of understanding and intellect is from You. Blessed are You, Adonai, who favors us with knowledge."

"Thank you, sit down please," he said.

Then it was Rabbi's Lieberman's turn.

"You probably noted that we are considering not only your performance today. Judaism means living your faith in your daily life. I have carefully followed your spiritual development over the last few years and am pleased about your progress. You seem to be committed and have taken the necessary steps to complete your conversion. I was informed that you intend to emigrate to Israel. Is this your decision?

"Yes, it is," I replied proudly.

"You are also aware that your decision to convert may deepen the conflict in your family. Remember that many people in this country still feel that you either can be a Jew or a German, but not both. How do you feel about that?"

"I know," I sighed. "I wish that I could have the opportunity to maintain a relationship with my family. I still honor and value their contributions to my life and upbringing. But I have to move on with my life and I know that this will be painful for them. But I do not feel that I am betraying my family or country. This is a spiritual decision, not a political one."

Rabbi Lieberman looked at the other two rabbis and they both nodded.

"Please stand up, Bernd," he said. He picked up a certificate and started reading.

He was reading in Hebrew, and at that moment I was too overwhelmed by emotion to understand the entire text. After so many years I had finally reached my goal. Now I was leaving my previous life behind and entering a new spiritual world, joining a different culture, embracing a different religion. I was trembling, and recognizing my excitement, Rabbi Lieberman smiled softly and continued:

"… And according to the Jewish law we as members of the Bet Ha-Din or House of Judgment, decide to accept you as *Ger Zedek*, a Righteous Convert. We reached the decision to accept you after a careful examination and review of your motives and performance. You are now as much a Jew as anyone else, and without distinction and are given the Hebrew name Dov Ben-Avraham."

I felt numb, as tears ran down my face. I remembered the mysterious rabbi I met at the HaKotel in Jerusalem and his words. Yes, a neschama had found its home in me and touched my soul. I was now one.

All three Rabbis shook my hand and embraced me.

"Mazel tov and congratulations," Rabbi Lieberman said.

"You are now a Jew and I hope that you have found your soul."

When I stepped outside into the cold December afternoon I was still overwhelmed by the events. I leaned against the wall of the building and cried. Then I slowly walked to my car and during the long drive home contemplated my next steps. So much to do, so many important things to consider. But I was ready to move forward.

Several days later I had to sit for my final oral exams. I passed them with honors and beamed with optimism and joy.

That same day I called my mother to tell her the good news, and she cried and sobbed on the phone.

"You should let your father know," she pleaded. "He needs to hear from you. Since your departure, he is drinking more heavily and does not talk to anybody. Please do it for me!"

But I did not talk to him then, and that afternoon I celebrated with my classmates. Unfortunately, I seemed to have inherited a high tolerance to alcohol and in the early evening I was sufficiently uninhibited to approach my father, but felt unwilling to meet him at home. My parents were having dinner at a local restaurant and I decided to join them. I was met with stares from the other diners when I entered, still dressed in my dark suit and noticeably under the influence of alcohol.

I found their table and approached.

"Just letting you know that I passed the exams and I am a doctor now."

Avoiding eye contact, my father tried to appear as cold as possible.

"That's good. And what are you going to do?"

"I will see," I lied. I did not want him to know that the same day I had forwarded via courier my conversion certificate and passport to the Israeli Consulate. Furthermore, I also notified the local office of the Jewish agency in Frankfurt of my intent to immigrate to Israel, also called *aliyah*, or to ascend. I would probably receive all documents and the immigration visa within a week, along with a one-way ticket on El-Al airline to Tel Aviv paid by the Jewish Agency. All those thoughts raced through my head as I stood before my parents, pretending I had no plans.

I knew that our relationship had already deteriorated beyond the point of no return.

We could not communicate, and I made no attempt to correct this.

The sad situation would continue to haunt me for many years, but at that point I did not have the strength to tell the truth.

I simply left the restaurant, knowing that this might be the end of our family relationship.

That same night I continued drinking with my classmates, trying to anesthetize my pain, but knowing that the next morning would be painful. For the next several days I stayed in my apartment, awaiting delivery of travel papers, and on the fifth day it came.

The postman rang the doorbell and I opened quickly enough to sign for delivery. I opened the brown envelope trembling with excitement. It contained my German passport, in which the immigration visa was stamped onto an entire page. It also included detailed immigration instructions and a one-way ticket from Frankfurt to Tel Aviv.

The departure date was only a week away. I had little time to prepare and to say good-bye to friends and parents. That week was filled with hectic activity. My parents could not fail to see that I was preparing to leave. One evening my father entered my apartment, unannounced as usual, and found me packing my backpack.

He stared at me, and then startled me by speaking in a pleading voice, at times almost choking in mid-sentence.

"So, you are leaving. Why the secrecy? I suspected that you would not stay here after your exam. Can you tell me what is going on?"

I hesitated, but decided to tell him.

"I cannot stay in Germany. I completed my conversion to Judaism and will leave for Israel to try my luck there."

He turned pale and took a step forward with outstretched arms, but then stopped.

"What can I do? What can we do to make you reconsider?"

"Nothing, father. Nothing can be done. I am going. I may come back, but I need time to find myself."

"I am losing my only son," he said sadly.

"No, father. We lost each other a long time ago, and I do not have the strength to start all over."

Looking at me with his dark brown eyes for the last time, he turned around and left my apartment without a word.

I was in tears. I wanted to call him back to apologize, to explain, but did not have the courage to speak up.

Now I was alone. Maybe I had gone too far to return, or maybe I was just too stubborn to consider it. Overwhelmed by that realization, I fell asleep and woke up late in the morning of my last day in Germany.

I left the house and walked into the city despite the bitter cold. The streets were covered by a thick layer of snow. I just wanted to take a final walk through my home town, passing the house I grew up in, the kindergarten and school where I spent my first formative years, and then the Jewish Community Center. Unfortunately, it was already closed and I left a note for Yaacov, thanking him for his support and promising to stay in touch. It was already getting dark when I returned to my parents home. They were out and I decided to go to bed because I had to leave early in the morning for the airport. I slept little, tossing fitfully in my bed, haunted by nightmares I could not recall when I was awake.

At 5:00 a.m. I decided to get up.

I knew that I could not sneak out the door, so I entered my parents' living room and was surprised to find my mother already sitting alone at the table with a cup of coffee. Her eyes were red and it was clear she had not slept. She did not seem to notice me until I spoke.

"Mother, I am sorry. I am so sorry, but I have to leave."

She finally looked at me and then stood up, but sank back into her chair. I moved closer and suddenly found myself on my knees, holding her hand and caressing her face.

"You taught me to have feelings and to be true to myself. I have done what I had to do to be true to myself. Yes, it may appear egoistic and selfish, but I finally feel at peace with myself. Please understand that I have to go."

She kissed my forehead and her tears dripped down my face.

"My sweet son. I am in so much pain to see you leaving. What will happen to you? You are so much like your father. Proud and stubborn. Filled with idealism. You will face so many unknown challenges and threats. How …," but the tears drowned her voice.

"Mother. I will always love you, but I am old enough to deal with my life. Don't worry about me. One day I will be back."

"Please say goodbye to your father. He stayed up all night in his study drinking. Please do it for me," she pleaded with me.

I stood up and walked towards the steps leading to his study. I just had to take a few steps to enter his room. But what would I do or say? I turned around in defeat. On my mother's face I saw only pain.

"I cannot do it mother. I cannot do it. I am not strong enough." Then I noticed the plate mounted on the wall above her head with the inscription written in old German letters: "Always forward, never look back." The last time I had noticed this plate was many years before, in our old house. But now it had real meaning for me.

"Mother, I love you, but now I have to go."

Shouldering my backpack I was about to leave when she stood up and walked toward me. Then we fell into each other's outstretched arms, holding each other tight, knowing that it might be the last time we saw each other.

None of us could know that we would have another chance, years later, to see each other. For now, I silently let go of her and left.

On the bus to the train station I tried to focus on the present and leave the past behind. But when the train left the station my throat tightened and my stomach seized in knots.

"This is it," I thought. "Now I have really passed the point of no return. Always forward, never look back."

CHAPTER 5

THE NEW BEGINNING

"IT'S YOUR WATCH NOW," Michael said, shaking my shoulder. I was already awake and silently cursed him, but it was not his fault. Michael and I belonged to a group of immigrant soldiers undergoing basic training in a military compound on top of a hill overlooking the Palestinian city of Ramallah on the West Bank. We had completed our first week, which seemed to last an eternity.

"Yes, I am up all right," I growled, noticing that it was four o'clock in the morning and my turn for guard duty. I'd fallen asleep in my dirty uniform so now I only had to slip into my army boots and put on my warm coat. The October nights were chilly and windy.

I grabbed my M-16 assault rifle, which was leaning against my bed, checked that the magazine was loaded and the safety on. I still had mixed feelings about carrying this rifle, remembering that years earlier I had been excused from military service in Germany partially because of my refusal to carry weapons.

Now the circumstances were different. The new Palestinian uprising, the Intifada, created sharp animosity and tensions. No more could I travel with friends from the kibbutz to Ramallah for dinner in those excellent garden restaurants. Now as a Jew one had to carry a weapon or avoid the Palestinian cities and villages altogether.

I picked up the gun and cradled it in my arms. I would have to stay awake for at least two hours before I would be relieved by another soldier. Stepping out of the barracks, I breathed in the clean air filled with the scent of pine trees. It brought back memories of the time spent in Abu Gosh with my fried Chalid. Unfortunately, he left for Russia to study medicine and I lost contact with him. Being a soldier now I hesitated to visit his village and I really missed him and our friendship. Then I began my sentry tour, walking slowly along a defined path. On these early-morning rounds, I had plenty of time to think about my life. Since my arrival in Israel two years earlier, life had changed dramatically. I had scrambled to adjust to the fast-paced life style and found that I enjoyed every minute of it. At first, my days in the kibbutz were filled with daily language classes and work. Then I completed an additional year of medical training at a large city hospital in Tel Aviv to qualify for my Israeli license. There I met an American nurse, who had immigrated to Israel some years earlier than I did. We fell in love and got married, and now she was pregnant with our first child. We already knew that it would be a son, which filled me with a combination of anxiety and excitement. Soon I would be a father, with the challenge raising a child.

As I trudged along the path, I was painfully reminded that my own father had died almost a year and a half earlier. His death had saddened and shocked me. Since my departure from Germany we had not spoken to each other, and I had chosen not to read his letters, lacking the courage and will. This was a decision I deeply regretted when I learned of his death. I had been trying to disconnect from my previous life and even my family, but when my mother sent word of his death, I felt the futility of my decision.

Several months after my departure my father was diagnosed with cancer and he chose not to receive treatment. He specifically instructed my mother not to inform me about his condition and died at home on June 1st, 1987. When I learned this, I grieved, and finally decided to read his letters. I was struck by his casual description of his life and my mother's activities, but he sent no reflections on my decision to convert and to leave Germany. I sensed that he still hoped that I would return, regretting my mistakes.

But I had stayed. As time went on the tone of his letters grew more aggressive and dismissive. In retrospect I realized that this was based on his anger and the realization that he would die soon. But he did not mention this important fact. The last letter was directed not to "my" son, but to "the" son. In a few sentences, he said that he was dying from cancer, did not expect any pity from me, and informed me that I was officially removed from his will. He said that he had only two last wishes – that I would not attend his funeral, and that I would refrain from sending any condolences to my mother. He ended the letter simply "Father."

Now, truly fatherless, I had to teach myself the skills of being a father from scratch. I was afraid that I would fail. I also knew that as my son grew up, I would have to face his questions about my family and especially my father.

In Israel, I was still ashamed to talk about him, and this attitude was already causing me problems in my adopted homeland. I didn't even tell my wife about my past, letting her believe that I was born a Jew and had emigrated to Israel from Germany.

Eventually, she found out, which deeply damaged our relationship.

Nor did I get any sympathy from the military. During my service, I had to undergo multiple security screening procedures conducted by the local field office of the military intelligence services. I was reluctant to answer questions about my family of origin, and this triggered further investigations. One day my commanding officer called me into his office. He was a colonel, but like most senior officers he maintained a cordial and relaxed relationship with his junior staff. When I entered his sparsely furnished office, I noticed a second officer with the rank of lieutenant colonel. His shoulder tag indicated that he belonged to the military intelligence unit.

"Bernd," my commander said, "let me get to the point. You are an excellent medical officer and I receive only stellar evaluations of your service. Nevertheless, Lieutenant Colonel Ofir has some questions that so far you have not answered."

I knew what it was about, and tried to remain calm. The military intelligence officer held a file in his hands: he was well prepared for this conversation.

As I expected he took over the questioning. He was a tall, muscular man, his haircut very short. His stern look stern was accentuated by his high cheekbones.

"Tell me about your family," he said.

"I guess you know about it already," I replied, already angry.

"I want to hear it from you."

"As you can read in your files, my father was a German Wehrmacht officer."

"Not just a Wehrmacht officer, but a highly decorated Tank Commander," he interrupted.

"Yes, he was the recipient of the Knight's Cross, one of the most prestigious honors bestowed upon a German military soldier."

"How can it be that the son of a Nazi turns out to be a Jew on an Israeli military installation?" he asked angrily.

I decided not to respond to the Nazi characterization, but to describe briefly my spiritual journey.

It did not seem to impress him.

"So you are religious, but you don't wear a kippa. Why are you living in Israel?"

"Because I feel strongly about this country and have wanted to live here for many years."

He stepped closer, his face close to mine.

"Military intelligence must know everything about anybody leading our soldiers. I have a hard time trusting a man like you. Convince me that you can be trusted."

I was shocked and deeply hurt by his attitude, and it took me a minute to gather my thoughts.

"I converted to Judaism, left my family, left my country. What else can I do to convince you that I am trustworthy?"

"I respect what you have done," he said, "but how can I trust a man who lied to his family and is unable to tell the truth?"

I looked him in the eye.

"Because I believed that it is better not to tell everyone the unbelievable story of how the son a Wehrmacht officer turned into a Jew. I still have a hard time dealing with it myself."

My commanding officer indicated to Lieutenant Colonel Ofir that he should stop the interrogation.

"Bernd, that's all for today. You can return to your unit and we will chat later."

My commander and I never spoke about this issue again. Even though I trusted him and his fair judgment, I felt hurt and stigmatized. My father was still a larger-than-life figure who would dominate my life even from beyond the grave. I had to escape his shadow, but how could I do so, and how long would it take?

Meanwhile, I had to deal with the full life I had chosen to live – in Israel, married, soon to be a father.

I also remembered with bitterness that even getting married posed a huge hurdle for me.

At the time my fiancé and I decided to get married we could not yet anticipate the difficulties we would face.

Israeli law does not permit civil marriage, but requires a marriage conducted by a Rabbi to be endorsed and sanctioned by the Rabbinical court. Any marriage has to be conducted according to the Orthodox interpretation of the Jewish law, or *halakha*, which excludes the marriage between a *Kohen*, or direct male descendant of priests, and a divorcee. Furthermore, the Rabbinical court will not permit or sanction the marriage between a Jew and one who has not been converted according to the Orthodox Jewish interpretation of the Halakha.

The dispute over "Who is A Jew?" has been waging since the creation of the State of Israel and Orthodox Judaism persistently refuses to accept any conversion conducted by Rabbis who are not endorsed or recognized by the Chief Rabbinate in Israel.

Little did I know that I would be caught in between the feuding factions.

I had been just drafted into the Israeli Army, undergoing my basic training, when I found out that my wife was pregnant and we decided to get married.

I asked my commanding officer to allow me to obtain a marriage license from the Chief Rabbinate in Tel Aviv.

I was still wearing my uniform when I entered the imposing, large grey building located right across from the Ministry of Defense in downtown Tel Aviv.

The ground floor of the building was bustling with activity. Dozens of bearded men dressed in black suits and wearing broad-brimmed hats were rushing from office to office.

Most ignored me, but some looked at me with unconcealed disdain for a soldier.

The majority of all ultra-orthodox men and women obtain a

deferment from military service. Most argue that the hardship of military service will prevent them from continuing their religious studies and that the exposure to the "secular" work will corrupt their values. Some even claim that serving in the military with women is forbidden like eating pork.

Religious men and women who choose to serve in the Army can combine their military service with religious studies. Men can serve in so-called *Yeshivot Hesder* units, specifically designed for the needs of observant Jews and women can perform national service in lieu of military service.

I approached a clerk towering behind a huge desk overflowing with loose paper forms.

Without looking at me he asked.

"What do you need?"

"I am here to apply for a marriage license," I responded.

"Do you have all the papers required for the application?"

"What papers you are referring too?"

At that moment he raised his gaze and looked at me almost starring in disbelief.

"Where are you from? Don't you know that you have to prepare all the paperwork prior to the application. That includes the proof that you are a Jew. Aren't you?"

I was stunned and maybe too naïve to immediately comprehend his question.

"But on my personal identity card it's written that I am a Jew."

He sniffed with disdain, pushing away the identity card I placed in front of him.

"We don't accept those papers here. They were issued by the Ministry of Interior. We only accept documents issued and sanctioned by the Ministry of Religious Affairs.

"Are you a Jew or not?" he growled.

"Yes, I am!" I proudly declared.

"Where were you born? What's your mothers name and where was she born?

Does anybody know her and her parents? Who are your witnesses and where are they?

Does a Rabbi know your family and for how long? Do you have any recommendation letters? I need ALL that before I can even consider your application."

I did not know how to answer him. Should I explain to him my conversion?

My father's past and the lingering questions about my mother's background?

Suddenly, waves of anger and frustration flooded my mind.

"Who are you, asking me those questions. I am a Jew like you. I am serving in the Israeli Army. It's written here that I am a Jew? "

His face darkened and he started to speak slowly.

"I need proof that you are a Jew. You either provide me with those papers or a certified conversion certificate. Are you a convert?"

The word "convert" pierced my heart like a dagger. I never considered myself as such. Yes, I had undergone a lengthy conversion process, but once it was completed I thought,

I was a Jew.

"Yes, I underwent a conversion, "I replied.

"Then we need to check the certificate if it is acceptable to the Rabbinical Court. "

As he leaned forward, he was wagging his finger in my face.

"If the certificate was not signed by an orthodox Rabbi, then you are not a Jew."

I could not contain my anger and emotions anymore.

"I really do not care about you and your rules. I am a Jew. I was recognized as a Jew. I am an Israeli citizen and I proudly wear the uniform of this country. If you refuse to issue me a license, then I will marry somewhere else."

I knew that an increasing number of secular Israelis were choosing civil marriage conducted abroad and recognized by the Ministry of Interior.

"The Rabbinical Court does not recognize civil marriage and the children from such relationships are considered illegitimate and cannot marry themselves," he remarked dryly.

Here I was. After so many years of struggle finding my spiritual identity leaving my life as I knew it behind, serving my adopted country and proudly feeling myself as a Jew only to be refused the right to marry and to start a family.

"I am and always will be a Jew. I will have children and they will be Jewish. They will marry and I will raise them to love and respect their faith and their country. You won't take that away!"

I turned around and left. I may have lost my trust in the Rabbinical Court, but I did not loose my faith. Several months later we were married by a Reform Rabbi and a local Israeli attorney arranged a civil marriage certificate, which was issued in Paraguay and accepted by the Ministry of Interior. For all legal purposes we were married and that what was important to us.

I glanced at my watch and noticed that my guard shift was almost over. I knew I had to walk back to the barracks, but wanted to enjoy the last moments of solitude. I stood at the highest point of the plateau, taking in the view over Ramallah and the adjacent Jewish settlements. I had mixed feelings about those settlers. The presence of the military base provided them some protection, but their relationship to us was tense.

Some of us, including myself, felt that it was not worth risking our lives to protect religious zealots. I understood their conviction that Jews have the right to live anywhere in Eretz Israel, but I also knew that those settlements were built on disputed land. The Intifada was fueled by resentment against those settlers.

The first rays of the rising sun illuminated the horizon. A steady breeze of cold air kept me awake and allowed me to enjoy the beginning of a new day. Today we would be leaving for Jerusalem and I was looking forward to leaving the base.

On my way back to the barracks, I passed a group of new recruits being lead by their sergeant on their morning exercises. In the barracks, our sergeant was already pushing us to get ready for the first bus, scheduled to depart at 8:00 a.m.

Needless to say, we were all eager to leave and assembled on time at the main gate.

We were instructed to load and ready our weapons because unforeseen road construction would force our bus to travel through the outskirts of Ramallah. I was among the few who had ever entered an Arab city or village before, and the atmosphere was tense.

Knowing the potential danger, I chose to sit in an aisle seat, even though the windows were supposedly impact resistant. The city outskirts reminded me of my friend's village of Abu Gosh – two- and three-story multi-family homes built from the same limestone. The streets were already crowded with people on their way to work, school, or shopping. As we entered a traffic circle, our bus slowed, and then it happened. We were struck by a hail of stones that shattered one window.

"Man down," someone shouted. I moved to the back of the bus to attend to the medical emergency. Michael was bleeding profusely from a head wound.

"What happened?" I asked.

"He was hit by a large rock," his friend Moshe replied.

"Open the trauma kit, remove a sterile dressing, and apply pressure to the wound," I said.

The stones continued to rain down on our bus and it was obvious that the situation was getting worse. At that moment our sergeant ordered us to leave the bus.

"Take your weapon, check that it is loaded, and follow the rules of engagement. Nobody fires without my command. Understood?"

We all understood and hoped that we were sufficiently trained to deal with the situation. Wearing my helmet and firmly holding my M-16 rifle, I joined the others and left the bus via the back door. I found myself standing on the main road in midst of several cars whose drivers had already fled. I moved carefully with my weapon pointed toward the roof of the nearby buildings, watching for snipers.

It may have been a trap; we had heard that school children were pelting buses and cars with stones to lure the passengers out into the open as easy targets for snipers. Or it may just have been children.

I stepped onto the sidewalk and approached a narrow alley. I was separated from the rest of the group by some distance when suddenly a young boy ran out of the alley with a large stone in his hand. He was about ten or twelve years old, with curly black hair that reminded me of the young boys in Abu Gosh who followed me calling "Almani, Almani, the German, the German."

But this time I was not the "Almani" but the "Yahudi," or Jew, occupying their land and entering their city. This time I was the enemy and could not expect any sympathy. Screaming profanities in Arabic he threatened to throw the stone. Almost as a reflex reaction

I pointed my gun in his direction with my finger on the trigger. My sergeant was pursuing another group of teenagers and nobody had given the order to fire.

I knew that I had made a mistake in being separated from the group. The sight of my weapon did not seem to intimidate the boy. He apparently knew that I had to follow rules and would not fire. We stood only fifteen or twenty feet apart and I felt a mixture of excitement and fear. Adrenalin rushed through my arteries and my skin felt like it was on fire.

At that moment, the memory of a hunting trip with my father flashed through my mind. We were sitting on a wooden ladder tree overlooking a field in front of a thick forest.

It was early morning and the fog lingered on the trees, reducing visibility.

Suddenly, we saw a deer carefully stepping out of the forest. At first I could see only his huge antlers and then recognized the rest of his majestic features. My father carefully raised his rifle and aimed through the scope. His finger touched the trigger and I felt the waves of excitement rush through my body – hunting fever, my father called it, ancient instincts that we still harbor in our bodies but only few of us experience. The loud blast of the rifle intensified my excitement and I cheered loudly when the deer collapsed, mortally wounded.

I felt that same rush now, facing the Palestinian youth. I told myself that this was different, that this was a human being. My instincts may have been appropriate for hunting, but this was no hunt. This was a standoff between two human beings.

We may hate each other, but we are created in the image of one god.

I also remembered that my father taught me never to aim a gun at another person, and my refusal to serve in the German Army had been based on a similar argument. Could I be true to that argument now? Would I risk my life for my ideals?

I decided to take that risk. I lowered my rifle and spoke to the boy.

"Go home," I said in broken Arabic. "No reason to get killed."

He stared at me in confusion then dropped the stone and ran back into the alley.

I leaned against a wall and took a deep breath. Relief flooded through me at having been able to avoid violence. I might have fired, even in the absence of a clear order, and could have argued later that I acted in self-defense. But I would never have forgiven myself. This was no battlefield. This was a Palestinian city.

These were children, and regardless of their dangerous behavior, they were not enemies.

Then I heard my sergeant calling us back to the bus. Noting my pale face he asked,

"Anything happened?"

"No, nothing out the ordinary," I lied. "I just chased some kids away."

"These are no kids. These are terrorists. Do you get it? They could have killed you!"

Still in the grip of my adrenalin, I could not hold back words that were sure to provoke him.

"I am not quite sure about that. This is their town. Their homes. Why didn't we take the road around the town?"

He stepped closer and stared at me.

"Are you one of those Arab lovers? Listen to me. Once you see with your own eyes what those bastards are capable of doing then you will reconsider. Now get back into the bus and stick to your doctor business. Obviously you are no good for fighting."

This time I was able to hold my tongue and quickly boarded the bus. Michael needed my help and I did what I had learned to be: a doctor.

Still, I was proud I remembered the teaching of my father, and I silently thanked him. I wished I could talk to him one more time, but he was gone. He had returned to what he called the "Great Army," the eternal assembly of his comrades, and fortunately he was still able to teach me from there.

I did not know that it would take me almost twenty years to find the courage to pay him a final visit.

CHAPTER 6

THE RETURN

ALMOST TWENTY YEARS HAVE passed and I am living a different life now. We left Israel in 1991 after the First Gulf War and moved to Miami. The missile attacks on Tel Aviv were too much for my wife. She worried about the future, and about our infant son, and she decided to return home to the U.S. I had to choose between my love for Israel and my family, and I was heartsick at leaving my adopted home.

Our marriage did not weather the challenges awaiting us in the U.S. and we divorced only three years after our second child was born, a beautiful girl. I remarried and was blessed with the birth of another daughter.

The years passed quickly. After completing a demanding residency program I am now a family physician and addiction specialist in private practice.

My work provides me with many challenges initially little time to reflect on my life.

Or so I thought until one normally busy day in the office.

It was at mid-morning when I was asked to take an important personal call.

"This is Doctor Wollschlaeger. Whom am I speaking with?" I inquired.

After a few seconds of silence a male voice, older, slightly nervous, with an undeniable German accent responded:

"Doctor Wollschlaeger. I need an appointment with you as soon as possible," the man demanded.

Without waiting for an answer, he continued:

"You were highly recommended by a mutual acquaintance and I am in a delicate situation requiring your assistance."

His direct tone and choice of words reminded me of my father's friends. He must have been a former German military man.

I felt a surge of discomfort, but was at first unable to identify its cause.

"No problem. I may be able to accommodate you right after lunch, around 2:00PM," I responded sensing that I would be faced with someone unusual.

I still did not know his name nor the nature of his emergency or problem and before I could ask, he hung up the phone.

Maybe he won't show up I thought, and continued my daily routine seeing patients, but my discomfort grew when the time for his visit came close.

The nurse directed me to the examination room and I picked up the chart, studying its content.

It was empty and the name was abbreviated as a single initial.

Entering the exam room, I was confronted by a tall and muscular man at least six foot tall, with white hair and some remaining blond streaks.

His eyes were blue and penetrating. He stood and greeted me with an outstretched arm. His handshake was firm, almost fierce. I asked him to sit down on the exam table and he reluctantly agreed.

I noticed his interest in the diplomas of mine and other honors, posted on the wall of the exam room.

"I see that you got around and collected several awards," he remarked dryly.

I was now becoming uncomfortable with this strange patient and tried to steer our conversation to the purpose of his visit.

"How can I help you? I understand that you have an urgent problem and you are seeking my opinion."

He sat upright and stiff, obviously reluctant to express himself. His posture reminded me of my father. He was in his early eighties, but appeared much younger physically. From his perfect German, I could tell that he was born in Germany, and I was tempted to ask him about those dreadful years of German history. Was he a soldier like my father? Had he known about the Holocaust? Did he participate in the murder and slaughter of innocent victims? It all began to play out in my mind.

I tried to refocus on him as a patient and to regain my professional composure.

"So tell me again why you are here?" I asked.

He did not seem to have noticed my short mental absence.

"I am restless and cannot sleep. I have these dreams and I cannot shake them off. I don't know why I am getting these dreams now."

His expression softened when he spoke, briefly revealing the features of an old man.

"Are there any recent stressful events that may have triggered those feelings?" I asked.

He hesitated before continuing.

"People are spreading lies about me, about my past, and it affects me."

"What kind of lies?" I asked.

He hesitated, looking at me.

"You were born in Germany after the war. What did your father do during the war?"

His direct question startled me. What should I tell him? Did he know about my father?

"My father was a soldier," I answered.

His eyes opened wide in surprise and admiration, which immediately aroused my disgust.

"You are a German who must understand that we were following orders," he said.

"I was proud to wear the uniform, but I did nothing wrong."

His reply increased my curiosity.

"What uniform are you talking about?"

He immediately resumed his stiff military composure.

"I was a young man when I was forced to join the 'Bodyguard Regiment.' His use of the German term 'Leibstandarte SS' made me shiver.

"Do you mean the Adolf Hitler Bodyguard Regiment?"

This unit was initially formed as Hitler's personal bodyguard and later morphed into an elite military unit comprised of ruthless fighters, who also committed heinous and terrible crime against humanity for which were few were held responsible.

He eyed me suspiciously and gave a dismissive cold smile.

"Your father has taught you well. You know your history!"

At that moment I wished I did not. He belonged to the murderous and infamous unit responsible for so many atrocities against allied troops and so-called "inferior races."

I tried to conceal my shock, but he seemed to have spotted it.

"I was very young and just followed orders," he added hastily.

His remarks opened the Pandora's box of my past. In his phrasing, I clearly heard again my own father's dismissive remarks about his past, his selective reporting of events he had so "proudly" participated in. I remembered how my inquiries about the past were met with silence or evasive answers. I thought of how my desperate search for answers had led me to Israel and then to Judaism. Suddenly my past had been dragged unbidden into my office – a past I had yet to deal with.

"Doctor, did you hear what I said?"

I tried to return from a distance of twenty years to this confusing conversation.

"Yes," I lied. "I understand completely what you are trying to say."

"So, tell me, why do I have those dreams? Why can't I sleep at night? What can I do to feel better?"

I was repulsed by his demands for absolution. Should I tell him about my other patients, many of them Holocaust survivors who wept in my office sixty years after their liberation from the death camps, still confined in their cages of fear and horror?

Their stories of unspeakable physical and mental abuse and survival told with tear-choked voices. Their eyes wide open, granting a glimpse in the abyss of their daily emotional torture.

Their torturers appearing in their nightmares adding eternal emotional suffering to their physical pain.

Should I tell him about my own struggle to find a spiritual home with peace from the hatreds of my homeland? Should I tell him about the lingering shame of being my father's son?

"There is only one way to help yourself," I answered finally.

"What is it?" he demanded impatiently. "Tell me! I will take any pill to get rid of this feeling.

"I certainly do not believe that a pill will help you."

He looked at me, startled.

"So what can you offer? You are the expert."

I reclined in my chair and looked at him for a few seconds that seemed to last an eternity. His eyes were blinking nervously as he tried to anticipate my meaning.

I said calmly,

"The truth will set you free, will liberate you from fear and allow you to forgive yourself for what you did."

His head recoiled as though he was being lashed by a whip. His eyes turned a dark cold blue and his face tightened into a mask. He spoke in a voice now distant and metallic:

"I did nothing wrong. My conscience is clear. There is nothing more to say."

He stood and turned to leave. As he passed through the front door he paused, noticing the little box or *mezuzah* affixed to the doorpost. It contained a piece of parchment rolled into a scroll and printed with a familiar text, beginning: *Hear, O Israel. The Lord is our God; the Lord is one. And you shall love the Lord, your God, with all your heart and with all your soul, and with all your might.*

He said nothing, but I could tell that he knew the meaning of this box, the ancient mark of the home of an observant Jew.

His visit did not affect me as much as the memories it awakened. There must have been a reason that his man, of all men, appeared in my office on that otherwise normal day. I knew that the only appropriate response was to revisit my own past, that only by returning to my past could I finally understand myself and achieve piece of mind.

I was reminded of my children as well who deserved to know my past and to have the right to form their own judgments about it. I needed to go back to visit my parents. I needed closure.

CHAPTER 7

EPILOGUE

REFLECTING ON THE PAST, I had lost track of time. It was already late in the afternoon and getting dark. My wife and daughter were waiting for me in the car and I was still standing in front of my parents' graves, reflecting on the events leading to my conversion and departure.

I tried to feel the pain my father must have felt at losing his son, and I forgave myself and him for our inability to communicate. A simple word, a gesture, an admission of mistake, an attempt to understand me – any of these could have led to a real relationship. But it was not meant to be, and now here I was, too late to heal the rift, but at last trying to understand.

Why am I here standing at my parent's graveside? Deep inside I felt the yearning to be united again with the father with whom I was walking in the dark German forests and who was holding my hand patiently explaining the wonders of this beautiful world around me. The father in whose presence I felt protected and safe. My thoughts were drifting in vain to a point in time where I still could identify with my father.

Why was I seeking closure?

I was tired of being fatherless. I had to accept my father as who he was. Accept his accomplishments and failures. His desire to raise a son to the best of his abilities and his limitations.

"Father, I am proud of what I have accomplished in my life," I silently said.

"Our conflict and struggle with each other has taught me to be a better man, and I am now. I am not ashamed and I am proud to tell my son who I am. "

But I also remember my mother who silently suffered in my father's shadow.

She wanted me to be so close to her, but then did not allow me to know her. I was unable to emotionally connect with her though I wished I could. Her life and her personality remained a conundrum to me until her death.

My mother, who always cared for and defended me, now lay before me in her final resting place. After my father's death she came to visit me in Israel, to meet my family and her grandson. I remember our emotional reunion at the airport in Lod. I had just returned from my army base; I was still wearing my uniform and my rifle was slung over my shoulder. Even so, she picked me out immediately from the crowd of waiting people. Her eyes lit up and we fell into each other's arms. I had not seen her for over five years and I was shocked at how much this frail woman had aged.

"Oh, my son. You look like your father. He would have been so proud of you." We both cried and held each other for many minutes.

During her short stay in Tel Aviv I recognized that her memory was fading rapidly and that she had forgotten many events of her past. She visibly enjoyed meeting my family, but she was unable to express and share her emotions.

My father's death had been devastating for her, as was my departure from Germany. Realizing that I would never return, she asked me just one simple question.

"Are you happy, my son?"

"Yes, mother, I am happy and you can be proud of me."

I offered to take her to Jerusalem, but she declined. In a fleeting moment of clarity, she tried to explain:

"I am too old and too frail to make this journey, even though I am so close. I cannot face the past like you did. You are a very strong and determined man and you have taken the burden off my shoulders."

"What burden are you talking about mother?" I asked.

"One day you will know," she said, smiling.

I never found out what she meant and until now have not investigated my ancestry.

So could it be true, I asked myself, that my mother concealed her family's past from everybody? Was there any truth to the rumors expressed by my late sister that we may have had Jewish ancestors? Would that have explained my unstoppable quest for answers?

May that explain why I was attracted towards the Jewish faith? Why I felt the spirit of the Jewish prayers in my heart and soul? Why I feel at home being in Israel?

Maybe the mysterious Rabbi in Jerusalem was right. My quest for spirituality may have been predestined. I was driven to find myself and by the desire to be reunited with my spiritual being.

I wish that my mother had revealed her secrets. It would have helped me to reunite with her.

After leaving Israel, I saw my mother once more, two years later, but she had already slipped into the silent world of dementia, never to be reached again before her untimely death several years later.

At the graveside it was nearly dark. Looking across the wall separating the Christian from the Jewish cemeteries I could see the tall gravestones towering over the wall with their Magen Davids placed on top.

"I have to go now," I said softly. "But I will come back and bring all of my children to visit you. You can be proud of me. I made it against all odds."

I put my hand in my pocket to feel the stone I had carried for so many years, the same stone I had picked up from a hillside near Jerusalem more then twenty years ago and kept as a memento.

"Mother, I have something for you that you always wanted to touch."

I pulled the brown limestone out of my pocket.

"I brought something from Jerusalem. The city I wanted to visit with you at my side."

I stepped forward and placed the stone on the grave.

The words of a poem by Yehuda Amichai suddenly formed on my lips,

"Neither the sound of prayer nor the voice of lamentation is heard there, for the dead praise not the lord."

No Lord, the dead are not forgotten!

I placed my skullcap on my head and recited the Kaddish.

"*Yitgaddal v'yitqaddash sh'meh rabba B'al'ma d'hu atid l'itchaddata ul achaya metaya ul assaqa yathon l'chayyey al'ma,* Exalted and sanctified is God's great name in the world which will be renewed and He will give life to the dead and raise them to eternal life."

One day I will be laid to rest here too. I may still be separated from them by the wall dividing the Jewish and Christian cemeteries, but at least we will be closer than we have been for a long, long time.

Rest in peace. One day we will meet again. One day.